INTERNET-LINKED
ROMANS

Anthony Marks
and Graham Tingay

Illustrated by Ian Jackson
and Gerald Wood

Edited by Jane Chisholm

History Consultant: Dr. Anne Millard

Cover photo credits: ... thanks to Arms and Archery

Contents

About this book

The city of Rome was founded in about 753BC. By 100BC the Romans had a huge empire that lasted for centuries. This book describes both the rise and decline of Rome as a world power and the way the people lived from day to day.

Dates

Many dates in this book are from the period before the birth of Christ. They are shown by the letters BC which stand for 'Before Christ'. (Dates in this period are counted backwards from Christ's birth; for example, the period from 100BC to 199BC is called the second century BC.)

Dates in the period after Christ's birth are indicated by the letters AD, which stand for *Anno* *Domini* ('Year of our Lord').

Some dates begin with the abbreviation 'c.'. This stands for *circa*, the Latin for 'about', and is used when historians are unsure exactly when an event took place.

Periods of Roman history

Experts divide Roman history into two main periods. The first is known as the republic, which probably began in 510 or 509BC. It is followed by the Empire, which began in 27BC when the first Roman emperor took power. Throughout this book the word Empire has been given a capital letter only when it is used to mean 'the period of rule by emperors' rather than simply 'Roman territory'.

How we know about the Romans

Roman civilization began more than two thousand years ago, but we have lots of information about how the Romans lived. Much of it comes from the sources listed below.

Many Roman buildings survive almost as they were built. They tell us about building technology and styles of architecture. Ruined towns, roads and aqueducts provide information on civil engineering and planning. Sculptures and mosaics inside buildings often depict scenes of daily life.

The Pantheon in Rome survives almost intact.

Shoes like this were found near the River Thames in London.

Buildings contain objects that the Romans used, including tools, utensils and toys. Some are well preserved, especially at sites where there were volcanic eruptions, because ash and mud have protected them from decay.

Fragments of pottery help us to determine the dates of Roman remains, as different pot styles are easy to identify and date. If, for example, experts can date pieces of pottery at the bottom of a well, they can roughly date other objects found in the same place.

Archaeologists record anything they find.

Many Roman coins are easy to date, as they depict events that are mentioned in Roman books. If found at archaeological sites, they can indicate when buildings were built or used. Coins found in places like India and Scandinavia suggest that Roman traders journeyed far beyond Roman territory.

This coin commemorates the Roman occupation of Egypt.

Much of our information about the Romans comes from their own writings. Very few Roman books or manuscripts have survived to modern times, but we have copies of them which were made mostly by monks in the Middle Ages and by later scholars. They include works by many Roman writers about history, politics and philosophy, as well as plays, poems and letters. These give us insight into the lives and characters of Roman people.

Other written evidence survives in the form of stone inscriptions. Details of laws, financial transactions and military records were carved into the walls of buildings all over the Roman world. Graves and tombs also give us details, both written and pictorial, about the lives and deaths of their occupants.

This tomb carving shows a Roman shipbuilder at work.

Key dates

On some pages of this book there are charts that summarize the events of the particular period. There's also a large chart on pages 88-89 that lists all the events in the book.

Unfamiliar words

Some of the words in this book may be unfamiliar to you. Some words are written in *italic* type, to show they are Latin (the language spoken and written by the Romans). You can look up the meanings of some Latin and other words in the glossary that begins on page 81. You can also read more about some of the people in this book, by looking up their names in the section called 'Who was who in ancient Rome', on pages 84-87.

Places

Small maps on some pages show where events took place. Some are based on a projection that may be unfamiliar. This has been used so that large areas can be shown in a small space.

Reference

As well as the glossary and other information, you will find an index at the back of the book.

Internet links

For links to recommended websites where you can find out more about the Romans, go to the Usborne Quicklinks Website at **www.usborne-quicklinks.com** and enter the keyword "romans".

The founding of Rome

The city of Rome was founded in the 8th century BC, in the country now called Italy. Most of Italy is rough, hilly country which rises to a central mountain range called the Apennines.

Some of the most fertile land is near the west coast, on three small plains around the Arno, Volturno and Tiber rivers. Rome was established on the plain of Latium, around the Tiber river.

Early migration into Italy

Long before Rome was founded, several groups of people migrated into Italy from other parts of Europe. The different arrows on this map show the routes these people took.

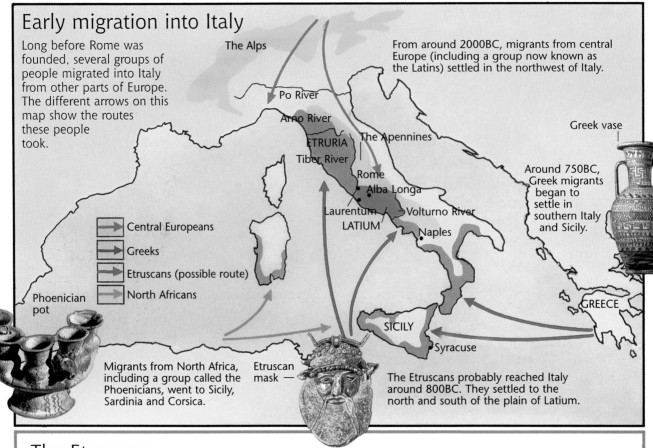

The Alps

From around 2000BC, migrants from central Europe (including a group now known as the Latins) settled in the northwest of Italy.

Po River

Arno River

ETRURIA

The Apennines

Tiber River

Rome

Alba Longa

Laurentum

Volturno River

LATIUM

Naples

Greek vase

Around 750BC, Greek migrants began to settle in southern Italy and Sicily.

- Central Europeans
- Greeks
- Etruscans (possible route)
- North Africans

Phoenician pot

Migrants from North Africa, including a group called the Phoenicians, went to Sicily, Sardinia and Corsica.

Etruscan mask —

SICILY

Syracuse

GREECE

The Etruscans probably reached Italy around 800BC. They settled to the north and south of the plain of Latium.

The Etruscans

Little is known about the origins of the Etruscans. They may have come from Asia Minor (now Turkey) before settling in Italy. Their civilization, based on a group of well-planned cities ruled by kings, flourished until around 400BC.

The Etruscans were skilled workers in bronze, iron and precious metals. They traded with Greece and the Middle East, and became very powerful and influential. At their peak they controlled an area from the Po river to Naples.

— The Etruscans made statues of warriors like this one.

These temple decorations, made of terracotta, are called *antefixes*.

An ornament on an Etruscan bronze bowl

The Etruscans buried their dead in elaborate coffins made of terracotta.

The first settlements

Rome grew from a group of villages founded by Latin-speaking immigrants about 25km (6 miles) inland on the Tiber river. There was an island there, and a ford where the river could be crossed. This was the furthest point that ships could reach.

The villages were built on seven hills; one of the first to be occupied was called the Palatine Hill. The villages were on important routes for merchants and so trade flourished. As they grew richer, the settlements merged into one town.

An early Roman settlement

Escape to Italy

Little is known of Rome's early history, so we rely mainly on legend. The date traditionally given for the founding of Rome is 753BC. The actual date is uncertain. According to legend, the Greeks laid siege to Troy (near the coast of modern Turkey). A Trojan price, Aeneas, escaped and sailed to Italy.

Aeneas sailing from Troy

Aeneas landed at Laurentum on the west coast of Italy. He formed an alliance with Latinus, king of the Latins, and married his daughter. Aeneas's son Ascanius founded Alba Longa (see map on page 4). He was the first of a line of kings who ruled for about 400 years. When the last king was overthrown, his twin grandsons Romulus and Remus were left to die by the River Tiber. A wolf found them and looked after them.

This statue shows the twins being suckled by the wolf.

A new city

The twins decided to set up a new city on the spot where they had been left. They held a ceremony to mark out the boundary, but Remus jumped over the furrow in mockery. Romulus was enraged and killed his brother, gave his own name to the city and became its first ruler. He was followed by six kings: Numa Pompilius, Tullus Hostilius, Ancus Martius, Tarquinius Priscus, Servius Tullius and Tarquinius Superbus. Parts of a wall around Rome, known as the Servian Wall (see map) and once thought to have been built by Servius Tullius, still remain.

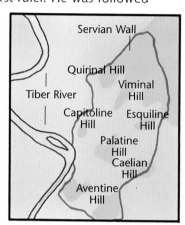

Servian Wall
Quirinal Hill
Tiber River
Viminal Hill
Capitoline Hill
Esquiline Hill
Palatine Hill
Caelian Hill
Aventine Hill

The influence of the Etruscans

For much of this early period Rome was ruled by the Etruscans, and under their influence it became a large city. But gradually the Etruscans lost their hold on Latium. Finally the last Etruscan king was expelled, probably around 510 or 509BC. After this Rome became an independent republic, but the Romans inherited many things from the Etruscans. For example, the Roman robe, called a *toga,* was based on an Etruscan robe, and the official symbol of Etruscan soldiers was taken up by the Romans.

The Etruscans built Rome's first drainage system.

The Roman *toga* (see page 42) was based on an Etruscan robe like the one on this statue.

The symbol of Etruscan soldiers, the *fasces* (a hatchet tied to bundles of sticks), was adopted by Roman soldiers.

Key dates

From c.2000BC Immigrants enter Italy from the North.

c.800BC Etruscans arrive in Italy by sea.

753BC Date traditionally given for the founding of Rome.

c.750BC Greek migrants settle on the southern coasts of Sicily and Italy.

510BC or 509BC Last king expelled from Rome; republic founded.

c.400BC Decline of Etruscans.

The early republic

Other cities in Latium formed an alliance and challenged Rome. The Romans were defeated at Lake Regillius in 496BC, and forced to join the alliance. Over the next century Rome fought many wars against tribes who attacked Roman territory.

Most Romans were poor farmers who had to fight simply to defend their land. By 400BC, however, after years of tough fighting and clever political tactics, Roman territory had doubled in size and Rome had become the dominant partner in the Latin alliance.

The fierce mountain tribes, the Volsci, Aequi and Sabini, attacked Roman farms.

The Gauls attack Rome

In 387BC the Gauls from northern Europe defeated the Romans at the River Allia and invaded Rome. Most of the people had fled, but the senators sat calmly in their homes. The Gauls stared in amazement, but when one of them touched a senator's beard, the senator struck him with his staff. A massacre followed. The Gauls destroyed Rome and only the Capitoline Hill survived.

According to legend the Gauls attacked the hill at night, but they disturbed some geese who warned the Romans of the Gauls' approach. Finally the invaders were bribed with gold to leave the city.

The Gauls attacked the Capitoline Hill by night.

Expansion in Italy

Slowly the Romans recovered from this disaster. In about 380BC they rebuilt much of Rome, and constructed a wall around its hills. By improving their army (see page 14), they began to regain lost territory. In 338BC, with the help of the Samnite tribe, the Romans defeated an alliance of Latin cities, making them the most powerful people in Latium. This map shows the position of the tribes in Italy around 338BC.

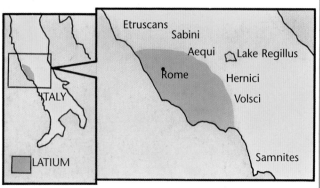

The wars with the Samnites

In 326BC Naples, in southern Italy, asked Rome for help against the Samnites. The Samnites objected to Rome's influence in the area, and a series of wars broke out. These wars lasted 40 years until the Samnites were defeated, along with the Gauls and Etruscans. Rome also defeated the Aequi and Hernici. By fighting hard and making clever alliances, Rome dominated northern and central Italy.

Samnite soldiers

The Pyrrhic wars

In 282BC Thurii, a Greek town in southern Italy, asked Rome to protect it from the Lucanians, allies of the Samnites. Rome did so, and soon other cities also asked Rome for protection. The nearby Greek city of Tarentum resented this and quarrelled with Rome. Tarentum was unable to match Rome's army but it had provoked a situation from which it could not retreat. So in 280BC it hired the army of King Pyrrhus of Epirus in northern Greece.

Pyrrhus attacked the Romans with 25,000 soldiers and 20 elephants.

Statue of Pyrrhus

Pyrrhus defeated the Romans in 280BC and 279BC, but vast numbers of his own soldiers were killed. He said, 'If we win one more victory against the Romans we shall be totally ruined.' This is why the phrase 'Pyrrhic victory' is sometimes used when a winner's losses are greater than his gains. Pyrrhus withdrew to Sicily, then returned to Italy in 276BC. He was defeated the following year, and in 272BC Tarentum surrendered. By 264BC Rome dominated Italy and was a major power in the Mediterranean.

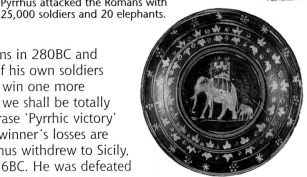

This plate shows a war elephant from Pyrrhus's army.

Colonization in Italy

When the Romans conquered an area they offered it an alliance, and drew up a treaty defining the status of the ally. Some places, like Tusculum, had full Roman citizenship. Others, such as Spoletium, had 'Latin rights', which included some advantages of citizenship. Others kept their independence at home, but Rome dictated their foreign policies.

All allied states also had to provide troops for the Roman army. In addition, Rome formed colonies of Romans or Latins in strategic places. By building roads and improving communications the Romans united Italian tribes. As the Latin language and the Roman way of life spread, the linguistic and cultural differences between areas were reduced.

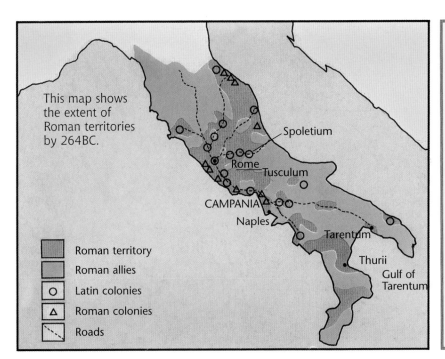

This map shows the extent of Roman territories by 264BC.

Spoletium
Rome
Tusculum
CAMPANIA
Naples
Tarentum
Thurii
Gulf of Tarentum

Roman territory
Roman allies
O Latin colonies
△ Roman colonies
Roads

Key dates

510-509BC Founding of republic.

496BC Romans forced to join Latin alliance after Battle of Lake Regillus.

By 400BC Rome emerges as dominant partner in Latin alliance.

387BC Gauls attack Rome.

338BC Romans and Samnites defeat other Latin cities.

326BC War breaks out between Romans and Samnites.

286BC Rome defeats Samnites, Gauls and Etruscans, and takes control of northern and central Italy.

280BC Beginning of Pyrrhic wars.

275BC Pyrrhus's army defeated at the Battle of Beneventum.

272BC Tarentum surrenders.

By 264BC Rome dominates all Italy.

The expansion of Rome

While Rome was becoming powerful in Italy, the western Mediterranean was under the control of the Carthaginians. Carthage, a city on the North African coast, was founded around 814BC by the Phoenicians, a people originally from the Middle East. Carthage was at the heart of a vast commercial empire. But in 264BC, a series of wars began between Rome and Carthage. These are known as the Punic wars, after the Latin word for Phoenician. This map shows western Europe at the start of the Punic wars.

The Pyrenees

Rhone river

The Alps

SPAIN

CORSICA

Rome

Cannae

Carthago Nova (Cartagena)

SARDINIA

Messana

Carthage

SICILY

Zama

Carthaginian empire, 264BC

Carthaginian empire, 218BC

Hannibal's route from Spain

The first Punic war, 264-241BC

In 264BC Carthage occupied Messana in Sicily. The Greek cities in southern Italy, under Roman protection, saw this as a threat. The Romans sent an army to Sicily and war broke out.

The Romans invented a drawbridge called a *corvus* which they dropped onto enemy ships so soldiers could charge aboard.

It took the Romans 20 years to expel the Carthaginians from Sicily. They first had to find ways of overcoming Carthage's superior naval skills.

The Romans had no experience of sea warfare, but they twice built huge fleets (see page 20) and won victories, then lost all their ships in storms. The Carthaginians were eventually defeated by a third fleet in 241BC. Under the terms of the peace, Rome acquired Sicily (its first overseas territory). Over the next ten years, Carthage had to pay the Romans a huge sum of money (known as an indemnity) as compensation for the cost of the war.

The Romans took Sardinia from Carthage in 238BC, and later seized Corsica too. They probably took this aggressive action to deprive Carthage of its island bases in the Mediterranean.

The second Punic war, 218-201BC

In search of a new empire, the Carthaginians invaded and conquered Spain between 237BC and 219BC. Hannibal, the Carthaginian general in Spain and a lifelong enemy of Rome, provoked the second Punic war. He launched a surprise attack on the Romans by marching over the Pyrenees in 218BC with 35,000 men and 37 elephants. He ferried the elephants over the Rhone river on rafts, then forced his way into Italy over the Alps.

Hannibal was a great general, and his troops won battle after battle. At Cannae in 216BC they destroyed an entire Roman army. Hannibal fought in Italy for 16 years and suffered no major defeats. However, he never conquered Rome itself, and the Romans remained defiant. After Cannae they waited until the next generation became old enough to form a new army.

Unable to defeat Hannibal in Italy, the Romans conquered Spain, then attacked Carthage.

Crossing the Alps, Hannibal lost nearly 10,000 men and all but one of the elephants.

Hannibal was recalled to Africa and defeated at Zama in 202BC. Rome then seized the Carthaginian territories in Spain. In the following decades the Romans conquered much of south-west Europe and became the major power in the western Mediterranean.

The third Punic war, 149-146BC

The third Punic war (149-146BC) ended with the destruction of Carthage. The territory became the Roman province of Africa.

The destruction of Carthage

The Roman conquest of Europe

Small states to the east of Italy asked Rome for protection, and larger ones pursued aggressive policies that led to Roman retaliation. Success in wars against Macedonia (215-168BC), and in others further south, increased Rome's presence in Greece.

In 146BC the Romans crushed an uprising in Corinth, destroying the city. The rest of Greece was put under a Roman governor. Soon the entire Mediterranean came under Roman control. The map below shows Roman territory by about 14BC.

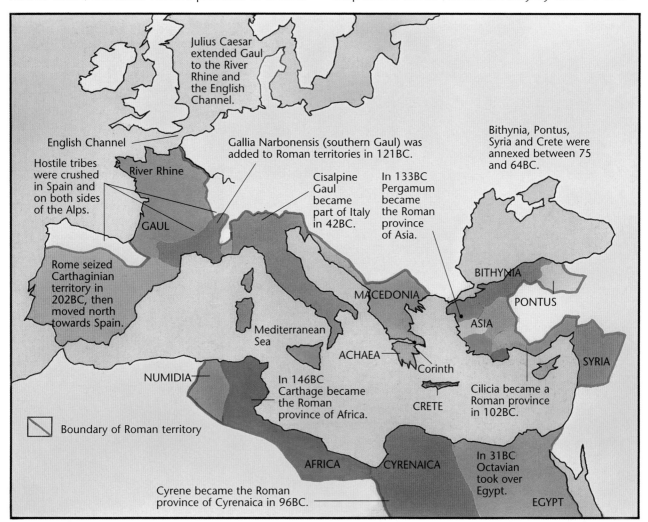

Julius Caesar extended Gaul to the River Rhine and the English Channel.

English Channel

Hostile tribes were crushed in Spain and on both sides of the Alps.

River Rhine

GAUL

Gallia Narbonensis (southern Gaul) was added to Roman territories in 121BC.

Cisalpine Gaul became part of Italy in 42BC.

In 133BC Pergamum became the Roman province of Asia.

Bithynia, Pontus, Syria and Crete were annexed between 75 and 64BC.

Rome seized Carthaginian territory in 202BC, then moved north towards Spain.

Mediterranean Sea

BITHYNIA

PONTUS

MACEDONIA

ASIA

ACHAEA

Corinth

SYRIA

NUMIDIA

In 146BC Carthage became the Roman province of Africa.

CRETE

Cilicia became a Roman province in 102BC.

☐ Boundary of Roman territory

AFRICA

CYRENAICA

In 31BC Octavian took over Egypt.

Cyrene became the Roman province of Cyrenaica in 96BC.

EGYPT

Key dates

264-241BC First Punic war.

238BC Romans seize Sardinia. War breaks out again.

218-201BC Second Punic war.

216BC Roman army destroyed at Cannae.

202BC Hannibal recalled to Carthage and defeated at Zama.

149-146BC Third Punic war. Carthage destroyed.

146BC Romans destroy Corinth as a warning to other cities. Start of Roman rule in Greece.

133-31BC Major expansion of Roman territories in Mediterranean.

31BC Octavian takes over Egypt.

Rome's social and political structure

Romans fell into two groups: *cives* (Roman citizens) and *peregrini* (foreigners). Citizens could vote and join the army; non-citizens could not. At first only those with Roman parents could be citizens. Later, some foreigners were granted citizenship.

There were three classes of citizen, as shown below. Non-citizens included provincals (those who lived outside Rome but within Roman territory; see pages 26-27), and slaves (see page 53). Women weren't counted as citizens either.

Citizens

Rich citizens, or patricians, may have been descendants of rich landowners.

Equites (businessmen) were descendants of Roman cavalry officers.

Plebeians (commoners) were probably descended from farmers and traders.

Non-citizens

Slaves were owned by other people and had no freedom or rights. The number of slaves grew later in the republic.

Provincials didn't have the full rights of Romans. They also had to pay taxes, while citizens did not have to pay any.

Families

The family was very important to the Romans. Every family was led by a *paterfamilias* (father), and included his wife and children, his sons' wives and children, and all their property and slaves. When the *paterfamilias* died, each of his sons became the head of a new family. The resulting chain of families formed a clan called a *gens*.

The *paterfamilias* looked after the family and led its religious activities (see page 62).

The patronage system

A client visited his patron regularly to be given food or money.

People who didn't have the support of a family (for example, ex-slaves) could attach themselves to an existing family. They were known as *clientes* (clients), and their protectors as *patroni* (patrons). The *cliens* gave his *patronus* political and social support in return for financial and legal protection.

The government and the Roman republic

Rome was governed by the Senate, originally a group of 100 men but by 82BC there were 600. Senators normally served for life.

Each year an election, known as an Assembly, was held to select senators to be government officials. The officials and their duties are shown below.

Eight *praetores* were elected, mainly to be judges in the law courts (see pages 74-75).

Two consuls (the most senior officials) were elected each year. They managed the affairs of the Senate and the armies. Consuls could go on to become proconsuls (governors in the provinces).

Four *aediles* looked after markets, streets and public buildings. They also organized and paid for public games (see pages 58-59), and could become very popular.

Each year 20 financial administrators called *quaestores* were chosen. They did not have to be senators to be elected. After 80BC anyone elected as a *quaestor* also became a senator.

Every five years two *censores* were chosen from the former consuls. *Censores* served for 18 months. They removed unworthy members from the Senate, and enrolled new ones. They were also responsible for making the state's contracts for public works and tax collection.

In emergencies the state could nominate a dictator, who normally ruled for a maximum of six months. He had absolute authority over everyone else. A dictator could nominate his own assistant, called the *magister equitum* (master of the cavalry).

Social change

At first only patricians could become senators. But many plebeians lived in poverty, and their resentment of patricians' power caused political struggles. The plebeians went on strike five times, threatening to leave Rome whenever they were most needed as soldiers. In 494BC, after the first strike, they set up their own Popular Assembly, which excluded patricians. Each year they chose officials called tribunes to protect their interests.

The plebeians held frequent demonstrations on the streets of Rome.

To pacify the plebeians, the patricians gave them the power to stop any laws passed by the Senate. The plebeians then demanded that the laws be published, to stop judges from using unwritten laws against them. A list of laws, known as the Twelve Tables, was published in 450BC.

The plebeians slowly won the right to stand for official positions. The first plebeian consul was elected in 366BC. In 287BC a ruling was passed stating that all resolutions passed by the Popular Assembly should become law. But during the Carthaginian wars (see pages 8-9), plebeian generals misused their power. Many people thought that only the patricians had the ability to run the country during the war. So the patricians still kept political control.

The end of the Roman republic

The expansion of Roman territories abroad led to problems in Rome itself, and placed a strain on the government. There were constant struggles for power between the Senate, the *equites* and the plebeians. A period of dictatorships and civil wars finally caused the downfall of the republic.

During the wars with Carthage, many small farms were ruined. Few farmers could afford to repair the damage. Gradually their land, and much public land, was taken over by rich landowners who created new, large farms.

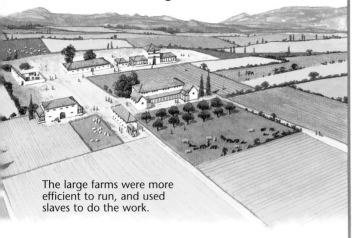

The large farms were more efficient to run, and used slaves to do the work.

People who lost their land either went to the cities, where they remained unemployed, or they lived in poverty in rural areas. As a result, Rome was short of soldiers, as only landowners could join the army.

Unemployed plebeians

Tiberius's land reforms

In 133BC a tribune, Tiberius Gracchus, proposed that public land that had been seized by the rich should be given to the landless poor. A law was passed and a committee was set up to redistribute the land. But many senators were landowners who wanted to keep their farms, so they provoked a riot in which Tiberius was killed. In 123BC his brother Gaius was elected tribune. Before he too was killed, he passed laws that challenged the Senate's power.

Political unrest

For the next 60 to 70 years there was constant political unrest in Rome. Some senators, called *optimates*, wanted to maintain the Senate's firm control. Others, called *populares*, claimed they wanted to spread the control more widely, but they really just wanted more personal power.

In 107BC Marius, a military commander, was elected consul. He was given command of an army fighting in Africa and soon won the war. He was made consul each year from 105BC to 100BC, breaking the rule that consuls had to be replaced annually. The reason given was that he was needed to stop tribes invading Italy from Gaul.

A Roman coin showing Marius in a chariot

Reorganizing the army

Marius succeeded in his task, but to do so he had to reorganize the army (see page 15). He allowed all citizens to join the army whether or not they owned land. The state didn't provide for soldiers without land, so when they retired they relied on generals to get money or land for them from the Senate. They were therefore more loyal to their generals than to the state.

Marius and his troops

A coin showing the head of Sulla

In 88BC Sulla, Marius's former lieutenant, became consul and took command of the army against Mithridates, king of Asia Minor. When a resolution was passed giving command to Marius, Sulla led his army on Rome and drove Marius into exile.

The struggle for power

As soon as Sulla had been called away from Rome once more, Marius took control. After executing hundreds of his political rivals he died in 86BC. Sulla returned in 84BC, destroying his enemies, and ruled as dictator from 82 to 80BC. He gave supreme power back to the Senate. He then retired, and died in 78BC.

However, Sulla's arrangements were quickly undermined by a general named Pompey. He won victories in Spain in 71BC, and helped the senator Crassus to crush a slave rebellion led by a slave called Spartacus. In 70BC, Pompey and Crassus demanded to be made consuls. Once in office they swept away Sulla's legislation, and gave power back to the tribunes.

Bust of Pompey

Pompey and Caesar

In 60BC Pompey, Crassus and a rising politician, Julius Caesar, formed an alliance. Caesar became consul in 59BC. After his year in office he served as a proconsul in Gaul for ten years. He extended Roman territory and became very popular. In 53BC Crassus died in battle, and a year later the Senate House was burned in a riot. To restore order, the Senate persuaded Pompey to become consul. Fearing that Caesar would return and take their power away, the *optimates* turned Caesar and Pompey against each other. They forced Caesar into civil war, relying on Pompey to win. Caesar led his army on Rome in 49BC, and seized power. He defeated the armies of Pompey and the Senate in Spain (49BC and 45BC), Greece (48BC) and Africa (46BC).

Bust of Caesar

Caesar arriving in Rome

Caesar's rule

Once in power, Caesar passed laws to relieve hardship, reduce debts and improve the administration. His rule brought a brief period of political stability.

Caesar was a great public speaker and a popular leader.

Caesar was made dictator for life. His reforms were popular but he acted as if he were king, taking decisions without consulting the Senate. Some people believed his power threatened the republic. On 15th March 44BC he was murdered by a group of men led by the senators Brutus and Cassius. They hoped to restore the republic, but Caesar's heir, Octavian (see page 22), created a military dictatorship which lasted for 500 years.

The murder of Caesar

Key dates

133BC Land reforms of Tiberius Gracchus.
123BC Gaius Gracchus elected tribune.
107BC Marius first elected consul.
88BC Sulla becomes consul, then marches on Rome.
86BC Marius dies.
82-80BC Sulla rules Rome as dictator.
78BC Sulla dies.
70BC Pompey and Crassus elected consuls.
60BC Pompey, Crassus and Caesar form an alliance.
59BC Caesar becomes consul.
53BC Crassus dies.
52BC Pompey becomes consul.
48BC Pompey defeated by Caesar in Greece.
44BC Caesar murdered by Brutus and Cassius.

The army

The expansion of Rome was due mostly to its army. The Roman forces were the best disciplined and among the largest in the ancient world.

The army influenced political life and many politicians were important soldiers. The structure of the army changed a lot during Rome's history.

The early republican army

During the early republic, in a military emergency, all property-owning citizens were summoned to the *Campus Martius* (Field of Mars, god of war). They gathered in groups called centuries, each of 100 men. At first wars only lasted a few days, so it didn't matter if men left their farms for a short time. By around 340BC wars further away from Rome meant that people were required to leave their farms for longer periods. Wages were introduced to encourage people to join the army.

Rich citizens could afford horses so they served in the cavalry. The rest fought in a block carrying swords, spears and shields, while the poorest fought on the edges with stones and farm implements.

Legions

Soldiers were grouped into units known as legions, each of about 4,200 men. Within each legion there were groups of different types of soldiers. These groups were known as maniples and they each contained about 120 men.

The diagram below shows the way in which the various fighters were organized in a typical legion.

Maniples fought in a special formation known as a *quincunx*, shown below, made up of three ranks of soldiers.

At the rear of the *quincunx* were 5 maniples (600 men) of very experienced fighters known as *triarii*.

Maniple of *triarii*

In front of the *triarii* fought a second rank, 10 maniples of *principes*, men armed with plenty of weapons and large shields.

The gaps in each line were covered by the troops in the line behind.

Maniple of *hastati*

Maniple of *principes*

Velites

Enemy soldiers

10 maniples of the youngest, poorest soldiers fought separately from the *quincunx*. They were called *velites*.

10 maniples (1,200 men) of young soldiers fought at the front. They were known as *hastati* because they carried *hastae* (spears).

In battle, the *hastati* wore out the enemy, then the *principes* moved through. The *triarii* only fought if a battle was going badly.

The later republican army

By 100BC the army had been reorganized by several commanders, including Marius. New laws meant all citizens were allowed to join the legion, whether or not they owned property. Wages were improved, and some men became full-time soldiers. Most troops fought on foot by now, but there was also a small cavalry.

Legions were well organized because they were made up of many small, highly disciplined groups. The main unit was still the century. There were now 80 men in a century rather than 100, because the smaller number was easier to manage. Below is a plan of how the legion was made up.

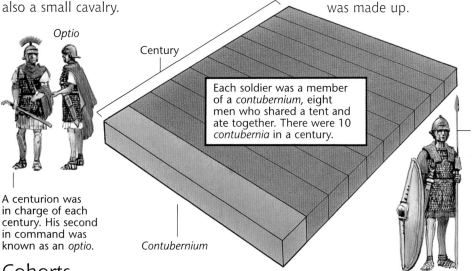

Optio

Century

Each soldier was a member of a *contubernium*, eight men who shared a tent and ate together. There were 10 *contubernia* in a century.

A centurion was in charge of each century. His second in command was known as an *optio*.

Contubernium

Each century had a *signifer* (standard-bearer) who carried the century's emblem.

To prevent the enemy from infiltrating the army, each century had a password that was changed each day. The *tesserarius* gave out the new passwords.

Cohorts

Centuries were grouped into units called cohorts. The cohort became the main tactical unit, replacing the maniple. Ten cohorts made up a legion. In each legion, one cohort called the *prima cohors* was larger than the others. It contained 10 centuries (800 men). The other 9 cohorts each contained 6 centuries (480 men), though the number of men did vary. The structure of a typical legion, with around 5,000 soldiers, is shown below.

Each cohort was led by a junior officer called a *tribunus militum*.

The *praefectus castrorum* was in charge of building and organizing camps.

The legion was led by a senior officer called a *legatus*.

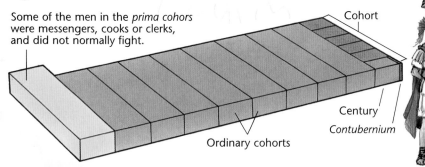

Some of the men in the *prima cohors* were messengers, cooks or clerks, and did not normally fight.

Cohort

Ordinary cohorts

Century

Contubernium

Each legion owned a silver eagle known as an *aquila*. It was carried in battle by an *aquilifer*. If the enemy captured it the legion was disbanded.

Other soldiers

Each legion was supported by *auxilia*, non-citizens recruited mostly from the provinces. These soldiers were organized into cohorts of 500 or 1,000 men. They were paid less than legionaries, served for longer, and were not as well trained. At the end of their service, however, they received Roman citizenship. They provided forces that legionaries were not trained for, such as cavalry.

15

A soldier's life

In early republican times any property-owning man between 17 and 46 could be called on to serve in the army. It was a citizen's duty to protect Rome. Soldiers were not required to fight more than 16 or 17 campaigns during their careers, but some liked military service and served continuously. By 100BC most soldiers were full-time professionals.

A new recruit took an oath of loyalty, at first to his commander, but later this was replaced by an oath to the emperor.

Each day new recruits did military drill sessions, and the entire legion exercised: swimming, running, javelin-throwing and fencing.

Three times a month there were routemarches of 30km (18 miles). The pace was forced at 6.5km (4 miles) or even 8km (8 miles) per hour. Legionaries were trained to build and dismantle camps.

Soldiers were flogged if they misbehaved. If a legion disobeyed its rations were reduced; if mutiny was suspected, every tenth man was killed. The word for this, *decimatio*, is the origin of the word decimate, which is still used today.

In difficult countryside, carts could not be used. Each soldier had to carry all his belongings, food, tools for building, two wooden stakes for the camp fence, and cooking pots. Because of this soldiers were nicknamed 'the mules of Marius'.

As well as learning to fight, some soldiers were trained as surveyors, engineers or stonemasons, and supervised the construction of roads, canals and buildings.

Under Caesar legionaries earned 225 *denarii* per year. Domitian increased this to 300 *denarii*. Soldiers had to buy their own food which took about a third of their wages. Meals were simple: cheese, beans, and bread or gruel made of wheat or barley. Soldiers drank water or *posca*, a cheap, sour wine.

Until AD5 full-time soldiers served for 20 years. Later this was raised to 25 years. The government knew that retired soldiers could be dangerous, and wanted to keep them peaceful. So discharged veterans were usually given a sum of money, or a small plot of land to farm.

Uniforms and weapons

A soldier's outfit varied little according to rank or status. New recruits had to pay for their uniforms out of their wages.

Soldiers wore tunics of wool or linen, and in cold weather wool cloaks and *bracae*, or wool trousers, were issued. Early helmets were made of leather but later metal was used for better protection. Vests of fine chain mail protected the body, and later soldiers wore the *lorica segmentata*, a leather tunic with metal strips attached. This allowed more freedom of movement.

Scarf to stop the metal from scratching the neck

Cloak

Chain mail vest

Tunic

A dagger hung from the left of the soldier's belt.

A sword hung from the soldier's belt by his right hand.

Groin-guard made of leather and metal

Soldiers carried two metal-tipped javelins to throw in battle.

Heavy sandals studded with nails

Bracae

Shields were made of wood and leather with an iron rim at the top and bottom.

Metal helmet

Leg-protectors, known as greaves

Making a camp

Roman legions spent many days on the march. When they stopped each night they set up camp, then dismantled it the following morning before moving on. The procedure was highly organized.

The camp was always laid out the same way. Josephus, a Jewish priest captured by the Romans in AD67, tells how camps were built in his book *The Jewish War*.

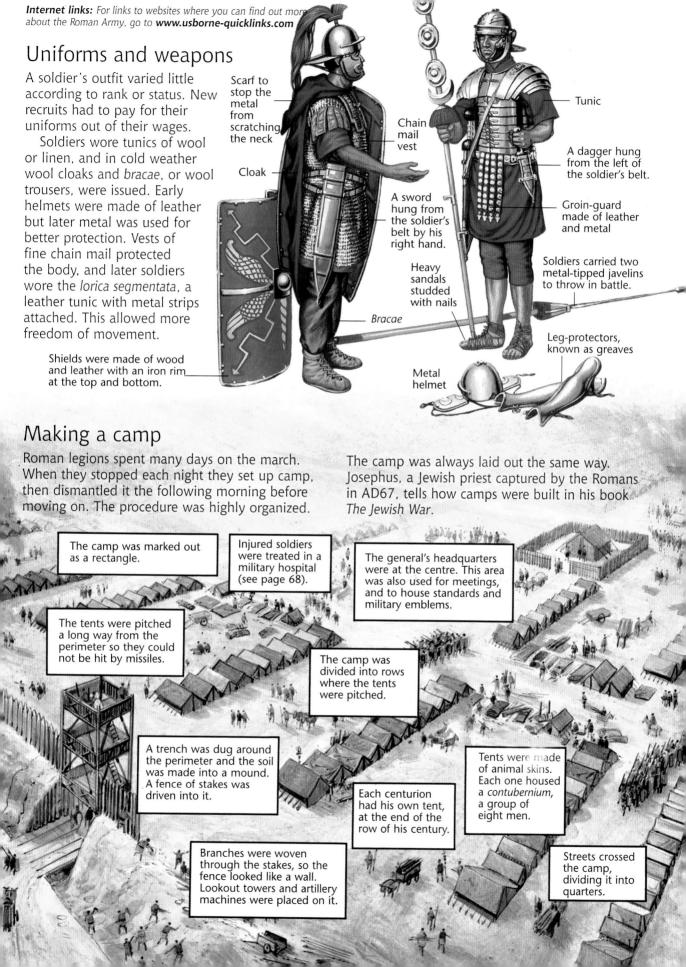

The camp was marked out as a rectangle.

Injured soldiers were treated in a military hospital (see page 68).

The general's headquarters were at the centre. This area was also used for meetings, and to house standards and military emblems.

The tents were pitched a long way from the perimeter so they could not be hit by missiles.

The camp was divided into rows where the tents were pitched.

A trench was dug around the perimeter and the soil was made into a mound. A fence of stakes was driven into it.

Tents were made of animal skins. Each one housed a *contubernium*, a group of eight men.

Each centurion had his own tent, at the end of the row of his century.

Branches were woven through the stakes, so the fence looked like a wall. Lookout towers and artillery machines were placed on it.

Streets crossed the camp, dividing it into quarters.

Roads

The Romans developed their system of roads out of military necessity. In the early years of Rome's expansion, the army could march from the city to defend the frontiers in a few hours. As the empire grew, however, it became vital to move troops and supplies quickly over very long distances.

The first major road, the *Via Appia*, was begun in 312BC. It stretched south from Rome to Capua and took over 100 years to build. 900 years after its completion, the historian Procopius called it one of the great sights of the world. He noted that despite its age, the stones hadn't broken or worn thin.

The *Via Appia* was the first link in a network that eventually reached every corner of the empire. Its remains have formed the basis of Europe's modern road and rail routes.

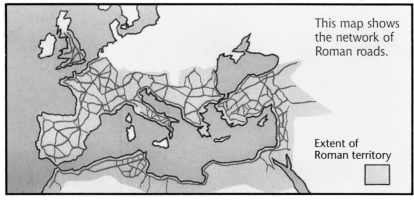

The *Via Appia* as it is today.

This map shows the network of Roman roads.

Extent of Roman territory

As well as helping the movement of troops, roads brought other changes. Merchants followed armies to sell to the troops, and later to the inhabitants of new provinces. Trade flourished, and people and goods could reach distant parts of the empire quickly.

On the road

This roadside scene has been reconstructed using information from Roman manuscripts, pictures and remains. We know what Roman vehicles looked like, and we also know their names, but it is not easy to match the two. Two-wheeled carriages, used in towns, included the *carpentum* and the more lightweight *cisium*. There were also larger, four-wheeled vehicles like the *raeda*, which could carry a whole family.

The Roman mile was about 1,500m (5,000ft), or a thousand paces long. Each mile was marked by a stone.

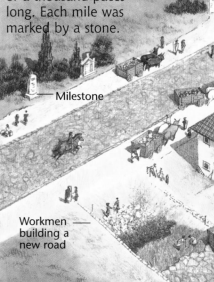

Milestone

Workmen building a new road

Building a road

When planning a road, Roman surveyors looked for the shortest, straightest, flattest route. To find this they took sights from one high point to another, probably by lighting fires, flares or beacons, observing carrier pigeons, or using a *groma* (see page 72). Once the route had been planned, the turf and trees were cleared. A trench was dug about 1m (3½ feet) deep and filled with layers of stone. To prevent puddles (which would crack the road if they froze), the surface was built with a raised curve called a camber, and ditches were dug to drain water away.

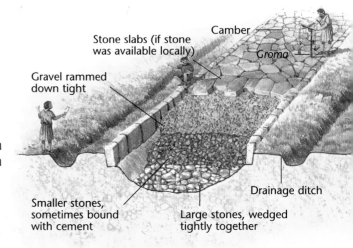

Camber

Stone slabs (if stone was available locally)

Groma

Gravel rammed down tight

Smaller stones, sometimes bound with cement

Large stones, wedged tightly together

Drainage ditch

Roman roads are sometimes steeper than ours because soldiers preferred a short steep climb to a long trudge around a hill.

Soldiers

Food and drink was served in a *taberna*.

Chariot carrying government mail

Coach taking passengers to the next city

Post stations on main roads were part of the *cursus publicus*, a postal service set up for government use.

Farmer taking vegetables to the next town

Guest houses, known as *mansiones*, were built every 15 Roman miles or so.

When the route came to rivers, or valleys that were too steep to climb, bridges or viaducts were built. Many of these can still be seen, and some are still in use, like this one at Alcantara in Spain.

Most vehicles had wheels set about 143cm (60in) apart. This width became standard once ruts were worn in the roads. No one wanted to have only one wheel in a rut, so they built their carts at this width.

One type of road, known as an *agger*, was built on a mound of earth. *Aggers* were up to 15m (50ft) wide and 1.5m (5ft) high. They were probably built as boundaries or to impress local people.

Ships and shipping

Unlike the Greeks or Phoenicians, the Romans had no tradition of seafaring. During the early republic they only had primitive shipping forces. However, for the first Punic war (264-241BC; see page 8), they had to acquire naval power quickly.

They found an abandoned Carthaginian warship and built 100 copies of it in 60 days; soon they had over 200 ships. After defeating Carthage the Romans dominated the Mediterranean Sea. They built a merchant fleet, and sea trade flourished.

Warships and naval tactics

There is little information about Roman warships because no wrecks have been found. We know from books that they were called *quinqueremes*.

These diagrams show warships and their weapons. Each ship had about 300 oarsmen, and 120 soldiers were carried on deck to fight.

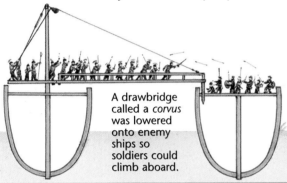

A drawbridge called a *corvus* was lowered onto enemy ships so soldiers could climb aboard.

Some ships used underwater rams to break holes in the enemy's ships.

Triremes

After the Punic wars there were no major naval battles, but the Romans kept a fleet of warships known as *triremes*. During the civil wars between Mark Antony and Octavian (c.33-30BC; see page 22) each side built up huge navies. 900 triremes fought at the Battle of Actium. After his victory, Octavian set up the first permanent navy to guard Italy.

This carving shows a typical *trireme*. The crocodile on the front suggests that the ship was from a fleet based on the Nile river.

Ports

When the Romans began using larger merchant ships (see opposite) they needed large ports. Rome was served by a port called Ostia at the mouth of the Tiber. Claudius built a vast new port, Portus, nearby. Ports were also built elsewhere in the empire. Towns grew up around them because they attracted plenty of trade. Barges took goods inland along rivers or canals.

Large merchant ships like this one brought supplies from other parts of the empire.

Merchant ships

After the rule of Augustus, the Romans had a fleet of merchant ships to carry goods to and from different parts of the empire. Surviving wrecks of merchant ships show how they were built.

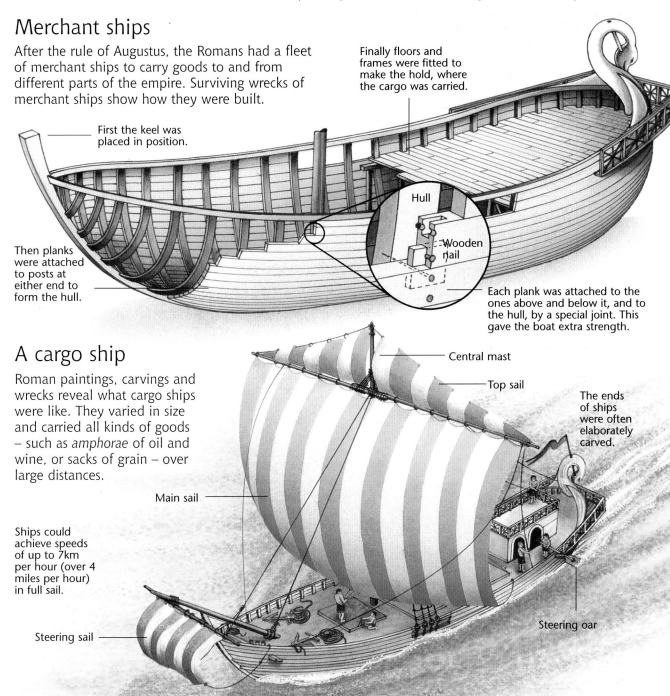

First the keel was placed in position.

Finally floors and frames were fitted to make the hold, where the cargo was carried.

Then planks were attached to posts at either end to form the hull.

Hull

Wooden nail

Each plank was attached to the ones above and below it, and to the hull, by a special joint. This gave the boat extra strength.

A cargo ship

Roman paintings, carvings and wrecks reveal what cargo ships were like. They varied in size and carried all kinds of goods – such as *amphorae* of oil and wine, or sacks of grain – over large distances.

Central mast

Top sail

The ends of ships were often elaborately carved.

Main sail

Ships could achieve speeds of up to 7km per hour (over 4 miles per hour) in full sail.

Steering oar

Steering sail

Navigation

Roman sailors had no instruments to help them find their way, but they quickly learned many routes across the Mediterranean. Books told them the best routes and best times to travel. We know from these that navigators did not need to keep the coast in sight as they sailed.

To calculate his position, a captain looked at the sun, moon and stars. He judged his progress by studying the direction and speed of the wind. There were lighthouses at important ports. The most famous of these, the Pharos at Alexandria, used huge metal plates to reflect the light of a fire. It was one of the wonders of the ancient world.

From republic to Empire

After Caesar's death (see page 13) Brutus and Cassius fled from Rome, realizing they could not restore the republic. One of the consuls, Mark Antony, tried to take Caesar's place. But many senators disliked him. One of them, Cicero, persuaded the Senate to declare him an outlaw. Antony was replaced by another consul.

A coin with the head of Antony

In the meantime, Caesar's adopted son Octavian formed an army of men who had fought for Caesar. He gave control of these troops to the Senate and they defeated Antony at Mutina in northern Italy. Antony fled to Gaul. The consuls were killed in battle, leaving Octavian to take command.

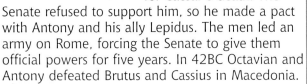

Busts of Octavian and his wife Livia

Octavian wanted revenge for Caesar's death. The Senate refused to support him, so he made a pact with Antony and his ally Lepidus. The men led an army on Rome, forcing the Senate to give them official powers for five years. In 42BC Octavian and Antony defeated Brutus and Cassius in Macedonia.

Octavian, Antony and Lepidus with their troops

Lepidus soon retired, leaving Octavian and Antony in command. They split Rome's territory into two. Antony took the eastern part and Octavian the west, as shown on this map.

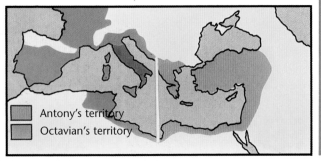

- Antony's territory
- Octavian's territory

The fall of Antony

Antony lived in Egypt for ten years with his lover Cleopatra, the Egyptian queen. Octavian defeated his enemies in Europe, and was accepted by the Romans. But relations between him and Antony deteriorated. War broke out and in 31BC, he defeated Antony in a sea battle at Actium.

This gem depicts Octavian as Neptune, the god of the sea. It celebrates his victory over Mark Antony.

Octavian takes power

Octavian claimed Egypt for himself, and became sole leader of the Roman world. In 27BC he offered to return control to the Senate and the people. He knew, however, that the Senate couldn't accept his offer because it relied on him to keep order. The Senate gave Octavian command of three provinces: Syria, Spain and Gaul. These areas contained most of the army, so he retained military power while appearing to want to give it up.

As a result Octavian became the most powerful Roman of all. He was given a new name, Augustus ('revered one'), and has been known by this title ever since. He was the first Roman emperor, though he himself did not use this title. The period of Roman history from his rule onwards is known as the Empire, to distinguish it from the republic before it.

This cameo shows the head of Augustus.

Key dates

44BC Death of Caesar.

43BC Octavian, Antony and Lepidus form an alliance and seize power in Rome.

c.33BC Growing hostility between Octavian and Antony.

31BC Octavian defeats Antony and Cleopatra at the Battle of Actium.

30BC Antony and Cleopatra commit suicide. Octavian seizes Egypt and becomes sole leader of the Roman world.

27BC Octavian becomes emperor and takes the name Augustus.

The rule of Augustus, 27BC-AD14

With his new power, Augustus began looking for solutions to his political problems. He realized that further civil wars would only weaken the empire more and leave it open to threat from outside. So he tried to make his own positon safe in order to maintain a firm leadership.

Knowing that troops could be turned against him, he cut the number of legions from 60 to 28. He used the wealth of Egypt to pay off retired soldiers, who were settled in colonies all over Italy.

A retired soldier

To protect himself, Augustus formed a division of soldiers called the Praetorian Guard. These highly-paid troops were formed to guard the emperor.

Under Augustus, rebellious parts of Spain and the Alps were brought under control. The empire was expanded along the Rhine and Danube rivers, The map below shows the extent of the empire at the end of Augustus's rule.

Praetorian guardsmen

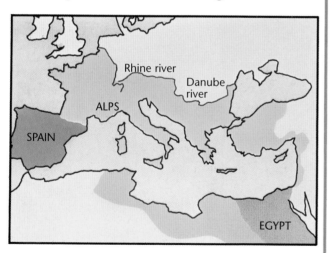

Augustus ruled very successfully. He formed a system of government in which the Senate and the emperor worked together. This brought peace after years of civil war, and turned a troubled republic into a stable empire. When he died in AD14, few people could remember a republican government that had been worth preserving, so the idea of restoring a republic slowly died out.

Tiberius AD14-37

Augustus had no sons of his own so he had to name his step-son Tiberius as his successor. The two men ruled together for the last ten years of Augustus's reign. Augustus disliked him, but Tiberius was a fine soldier and an experienced administrator.

Statue of Tiberius

At first Tiberius ruled well. But he was terrified of being assassinated and Sejanus, the commander of the Praetorian Guard, took advantage of his fears.

In AD26 Sejanus persuaded Tiberius to move to the island of Capri for his own safety. For the rest of his rule, the Senate had to consult him by letter. In AD31 Tiberius found out that Sejanus was planning to dispose of him. He revealed this to the Senate and Sejanus and his family were executed. This left Tiberius mentally disturbed. He passed a treason law and prosecuted over 100 leading figures. 65 of these were executed or committed suicide.

Gaius (Caligula) AD37-41

Gaius is often known as Caligula, a nickname he was given as a child because of the little soldier's boots (*caligulae*) he wore. After a few months in power he had an illness which appears to have left him deranged. He claimed to be a god and tried to have his horse elected consul. He also married his sister and later killed her. Gaius became very unpopular and was eventually murdered by a group of officers from the Praetorian Guard.

Gaius tried to have his horse elected consul.

The murder of Gaius by the Praetorian Guard

The early Empire

Claudius AD41-54

Claudius was Tiberius's nephew. A childhood disease had left him crippled, frail and nervous. His family and the Senate regarded him as stupid, and everyone thought he was not suitable to

Coin with head of Claudius

be emperor. After Gaius's murder, however, the Praetorian Guard found Claudius hiding in the palace. They dragged him off, hailing him as the new emperor. The senators resented Claudius because he had been appointed against their will.

Claudius being dragged off by the Praetorian Guard.

Claudius was, in fact, highly intelligent. He improved the civil service and extended the empire. He also ordered the invasion of Britain. It is thought that his fourth and last wife, his niece Agrippina, poisoned him so that Nero, her son by a previous marriage, could become emperor.

Nero AD54-68

Nero was only 16 when he became emperor. For the first years of his rule he ruled sensibly. However, he soon became tyrannical. In AD59 he had his mother, his wife and Claudius's son Britannicus murdered. Soon, anyone who opposed him was killed.

Nero took part in theatrical shows, races and games. This was thought to be undignified.

In AD64 a fire devastated Rome. It was thought that Nero started it so that he could build a new city. Nero blamed the Christians for the fire, and had many of them burned or thrown to the wild beasts.

Nero is thought to have played the lyre while Rome burned.

In AD68 the army rebelled against Nero and various commanders tried to seize power. Nero eventually left Rome, and he committed suicide. He was the last emperor of Augustus's dynasty.

AD69: the year of the four emperors

After Nero's death, an army commander named Galba took power. But he did not pay the guardsmen enough to win their loyalty. They soon had him murdered, and replaced him with Otho, the governor of a province in Spain. Hearing this, the legions on the Rhine declared Vitellius, their own general, emperor. They marched on Rome and defeated Otho. Then legions on the Danube decided their general, Vespasian, should be emperor. He marched on Rome and killed Vitellius.

Coin with the head of Vespasian

Vespasian (AD69-79) and the Flavian Dynasty

Vespasian established good relations with the Senate and they granted him imperial power. He also had two sons to take over after his death, so he had a strong line of succession. Vespasian ruled well and gave citizenship to many people in the provinces. His full name was Titus Flavius Vespasianus, and he and his descendants are known as the Flavian Dynasty.

Vespasian ordered the building of the Colosseum in Rome. This is how it looks today.

Titus AD79-81

Vespasian's son Titus is remembered for his capture of Jerusalem in AD70, commemorated by an arch in Rome.

The arch of Titus

Domitian AD81-96

Domitian, Titus's younger brother, was an efficient but arrogant emperor. His rule became tyrannical, and he was assassinated in AD96.

This was probably the last point at which the Romans could have restored a republican government. But the Senate, knowing that Rome needed a strong leader, chose a lawyer called Nerva to replace Domitian. Nerva was the first of a group of rulers known as the Five Good Emperors.

Bust of Domitian

Nerva AD96-98

Nerva ruled successfully and diplomatically. When the Praetorian Guard was indignant at having no say in choosing the emperor, Nerva eased the situation by adopting a famous soldier named Trajan as his son, partner and successor. This started a new method of imperial succession. After Nerva each emperor, who took the title Augustus, chose a younger colleague called the Caesar as his heir. When the Augustus died, the Caesar took his position and title, and then chose his own Caesar.

The imperial succession:

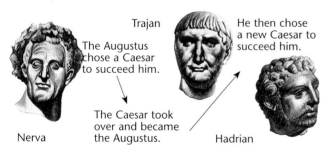

Trajan

Nerva

The Augustus chose a Caesar to succeed him.

The Caesar took over and became the Augustus.

He then chose a new Caesar to succeed him.

Hadrian

Nerva treated the Senate with great respect, and this trend was followed by the next four emperors. Gradually senators were chosen from all over the empire. Nerva also arranged low-interest loans for farmers. The interest from these was used to support orphans and poor children.

Trajan AD98-117

Under Trajan the empire reached its largest extent after his conquest of large areas of the Middle East. His campaigns in Dacia (modern Romania) are recorded in a series of sculptures on the pillar in Rome known as Trajan's Column.

Trajan's column

Hadrian AD117-138

Hadrian spent over half his rule touring the provinces. After deciding that the empire was too large, he gave up the new territories in the East (except Dacia). He also ordered the building of fortified barriers in Britain and Germany to protect the empire.

Hadrian's Wall in Britain (see pages 28-29)

Antoninus Pius AD138-161

While Antoninus Pius ruled, Rome was seen to be at the height of its wealth and power. This aroused the envy of the barbarians, and the neglected poor.

Marcus Aurelius AD161-180

Marcus Aurelius spent most of his rule trying to keep barbarians out. He had to enlarge the army and raise taxes to cover the cost. During his rule a plague killed thousands. People soon began to doubt that Rome was all-powerful.

This statue of Marcus Aurelius once stood on the Capitoline Hill.

Key dates: the first emperors

27BC-AD14 Augustus	**AD69-79** Vespasian
AD14-37 Tiberius	**AD79-81** Titus
AD37-41 Gaius (Caligula)	**AD81-96** Domitian
AD41-54 Claudius	**AD96-98** Nerva
AD54-68 Nero	**AD98-117** Trajan
AD64 Great fire of Rome.	**AD117-138** Hadrian
AD69 Year of the four emperors.	**AD138-161** Antoninus Pius
	AD161-180 Marcus Aurelius

The administration of the empire

Roman territory was divided into areas known as provinces. These were governed locally by senators. When a province was made part of the empire, a special provincial law was drawn up for it. This differed from the law in Rome, because it took local customs into account. After this, provincials were mostly left to govern themselves. This map* indicates the extent of the empire at its largest, under Trajan (AD98-117), and shows how it was organized.

Barbarians

Outside the empire were many rural tribes. The Romans saw them as inferior and uncivilized, and referred to them as barbarians. Some barbarian tribes wanted to regain territory, others wanted to steal cattle and other goods. To keep them out, the Romans built walls along some of their borders. These are shown as blue lines.

Most of western Europe was inhabited by rural tribes and nomads. The Romans built large towns there, to make it easier to govern and also because they believed urban life was a good thing. Most towns roughly followed the plan shown here.

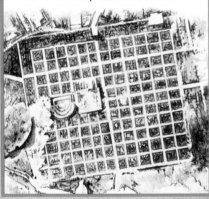

Caledonia
BRITANNIA
GERMANIA
Germania inferior
Belgica
Rhaetia
Noricum
Dacia
Lugdunensis
Germania superior
Pannonia
Alpes Penninae
Illyricum
GALLIA
Dalmatia
Alpes Cottiae
Adriatic Sea
Atlantic Ocean
Aquitania
Rome
Macedonia
Narbonensis
Alpes Maritimae
Corsica
ITALIA
Epirus
Tarraconensis
GRAECIA
HISPANIA
Sardinia
Sicilia
Achaea
Lusitania
Mediterranean Sea
Baetica
Africa
MAURETANIA Numidia
Caesariensis
Tingitana
AFRICA

The imperial army

When Augustus took power in 31BC the army consisted of 60 legions. He cut this number to 28. Later emperors varied this number slightly, but there were always around 30. Hadrian began recruiting soldiers from areas in which they would be stationed. For example, German troops were recruited to serve in Germany.

German soldier

Gradually the army became inefficient. Some later emperors thought the legions might turn against them, and to prevent this they gave soldiers special privileges and frequent pay increases. This made generals too powerful, and caused discipline problems. It became harder to recruit soldiers, because fewer people wanted to join the army. Sometimes barbarians were recruited but their loyalty could not be guaranteed.

*For a note about the projection of this map, see page 3.

Most eastern Mediterranean countries had a civilization much older than Rome's. Many had been influenced by Greek civilization. They were urban societies, used to central government and paying taxes.

Many Roman buildings were copied from Greek temples like this one.

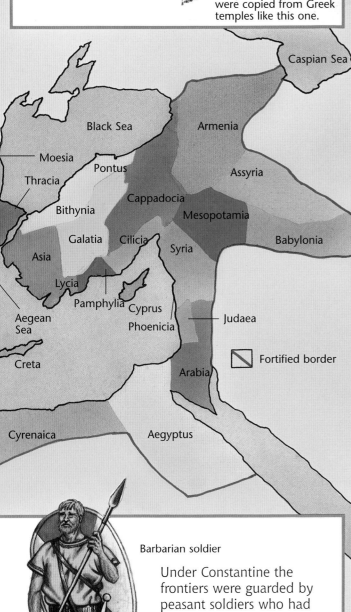

Caspian Sea

Black Sea

Armenia

Moesia

Pontus

Thracia

Assyria

Bithynia

Cappadocia

Mesopotamia

Galatia

Cilicia

Syria

Babylonia

Asia

Lycia

Pamphylia

Cyprus

Judaea

Aegean Sea

Phoenicia

Creta

☒ Fortified border

Arabia

Cyrenaica

Aegyptus

Barbarian soldier

Under Constantine the frontiers were guarded by peasant soldiers who had settled near forts. To support them Constantine organized mobile armies which were stationed near the borders. This worked for over a century, but finally the army disintegrated and barbarians moved in (see pages 78-79).

Government in the provinces

Under the republic, the Senate appointed governors for each province. They were chosen from retiring *praetores* and consuls, and served for one to three years. Governors had various duties. They commanded the army in the area, ensuring that frontiers were safe and maintaining law and order. They organized the collection of local taxes, which were used to pay the army stationed in the area. They also acted as judges for important trials. Governors were paid expenses, but no wages. Many, believing they would not be found out by the Senate, used their power to extort money from locals. For this reason they were often disliked.

The governor was helped by a *quaestor*, a junior official who collected taxes.

There were also three or four lieutenants (known as *legati*) who carried out the governor's orders.

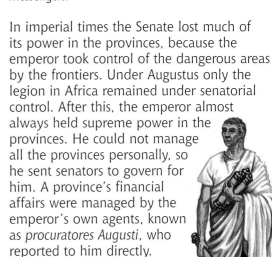

Civil servants called *apparitores* worked as clerks and messengers.

In imperial times the Senate lost much of its power in the provinces, because the emperor took control of the dangerous areas by the frontiers. Under Augustus only the legion in Africa remained under senatorial control. After this, the emperor almost always held supreme power in the provinces. He could not manage all the provinces personally, so he sent senators to govern for him. A province's financial affairs were managed by the emperor's own agents, known as *procuratores Augusti*, who reported to him directly.

Procuratores Augusti were a useful check on the governor's actions.

Sieges and fortifications

The Romans were determined fighters. They even conquered towns that were protected by high walls. Sometimes the Romans surrounded towns. The inhabitants, unable to get in or out, were starved of food and had to surrender. But the Romans also invented ways of ending sieges more quickly.

Roman soldiers used heavy weapons, or artillery, known as *tormenta*. These machines could fire missiles over long distances. They also built siege-works – wooden scaffolding and platforms that enabled them to climb the walls. This is what a siege might have looked like.

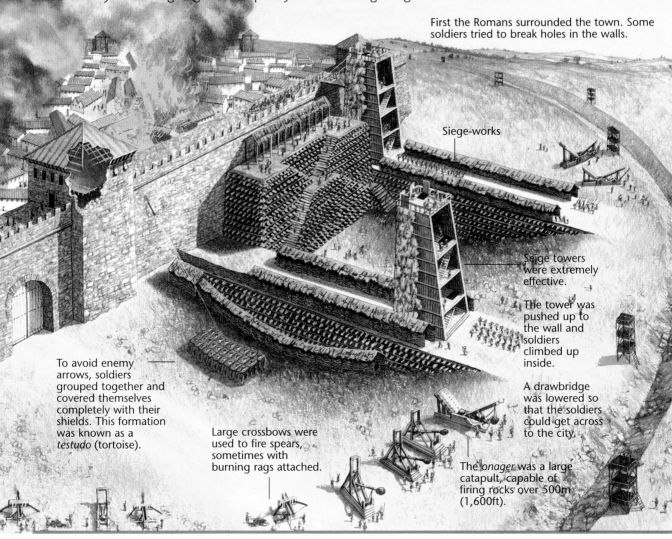

First the Romans surrounded the town. Some soldiers tried to break holes in the walls.

Siege-works

Seige towers were extremely effective.

The tower was pushed up to the wall and soldiers climbed up inside.

A drawbridge was lowered so that the soldiers could get across to the city.

To avoid enemy arrows, soldiers grouped together and covered themselves completely with their shields. This formation was known as a *testudo* (tortoise).

Large crossbows were used to fire spears, sometimes with burning rags attached.

The *onager* was a large catapult, capable of firing rocks over 500m (1,600ft).

Permanent fortifications

Hadrian wanted permanent frontiers at the borders of the empire. Walls were built in Germany, Numidia and Britain. The one in Britain, known as Hadrian's Wall, is the best preserved. It was built by soldiers in the three British legions, mainly between AD122 and AD129. It runs for nearly 130km (80 miles).It was not only a barrier, like a city wall. It also had a political function, enabling the Romans to control the tribes to the north. This is a reconstruction of part of Hadrian's Wall.

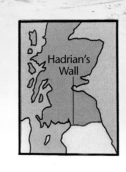

Hadrian's Wall

16 large forts were spaced out along the wall. Each one housed 1,000 men, or a cavalry division of 500 men and their horses.

The wall was built by soldiers of the British legions, but staffed by *auxilia* (see page 15).

Maintaining frontiers

When legions settled at frontiers they set up permanent camps, laid out like the temporary ones that soldiers built when they were on the march (see page 17). Each one held about 5,000 people.

Camps followed a similar plan so they were familiar to soldiers wherever they were. At first soldiers lived in tents, later in wooden huts. In the 2nd century AD stone forts were built, like the one below.

1 *Principia* (headquarters)

2 *Praetorium* (commander's house)

3 Barrack blocks

4 Granaries

5 Drill hall

6 Workshop

7 Houses for officers

8 Barrack blocks for first cohort

9 Cavalry accommodation

10 Houses for centurions of first cohort

11 House for senior centurion

12 *Valetudinarium* (hospital)

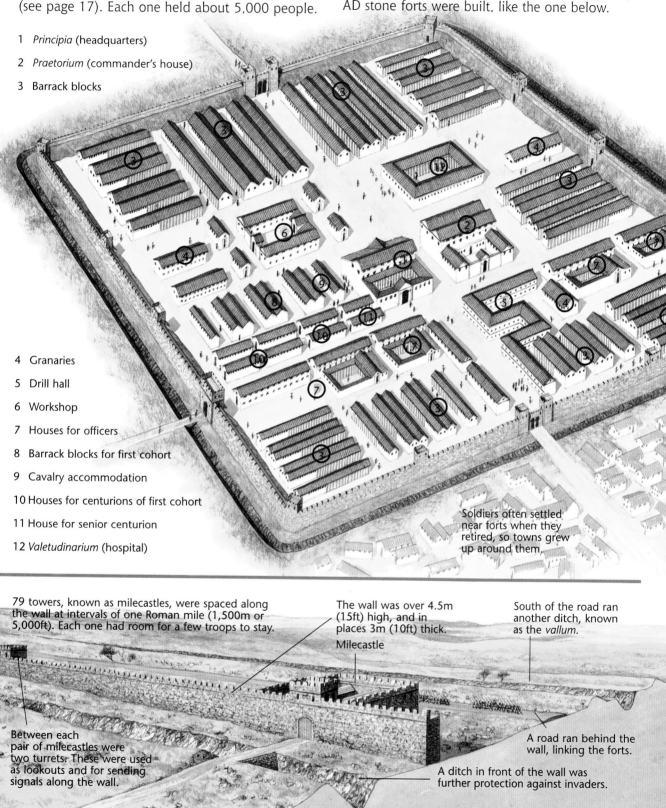

Soldiers often settled near forts when they retired, so towns grew up around them.

79 towers, known as milecastles, were spaced along the wall at intervals of one Roman mile (1,500m or 5,000ft). Each one had room for a few troops to stay.

The wall was over 4.5m (15ft) high, and in places 3m (10ft) thick.

Milecastle

South of the road ran another ditch, known as the *vallum*.

Between each pair of milecastles were two turrets. These were used as lookouts and for sending signals along the wall.

A road ran behind the wall, linking the forts.

A ditch in front of the wall was further protection against invaders.

Internet links: *For links to websites where you can find out more about Roman towns and take a virtual tour of Pompeii, go to* **www.usborne-quicklinks.com**

Roman towns

Early Roman towns had no particular plan or design, unlike many Greek cities which were built on a grid pattern with streets at right angles to each other. This idea had been introduced around 450BC by the Greek town planner Hippodamus.

When the Romans occupied Greek cities in southern Italy around 250BC, they adopted the grid pattern for themselves. To it they added the features of the Roman town – the *forum*, basilicas, amphitheatres, baths, drains and water systems.

Many provincial towns that existed before the Romans occupied them had defensive walls. During the early empire, when these towns were protected by the army, walls were no longer needed. New towns were forbidden to build them.

Later, however, when invaders threatened the empire, earthworks were permitted. Many of these were later made into stone walls.

This is a reconstruction of a typical Roman town. The basic features became standard throughout the empire.

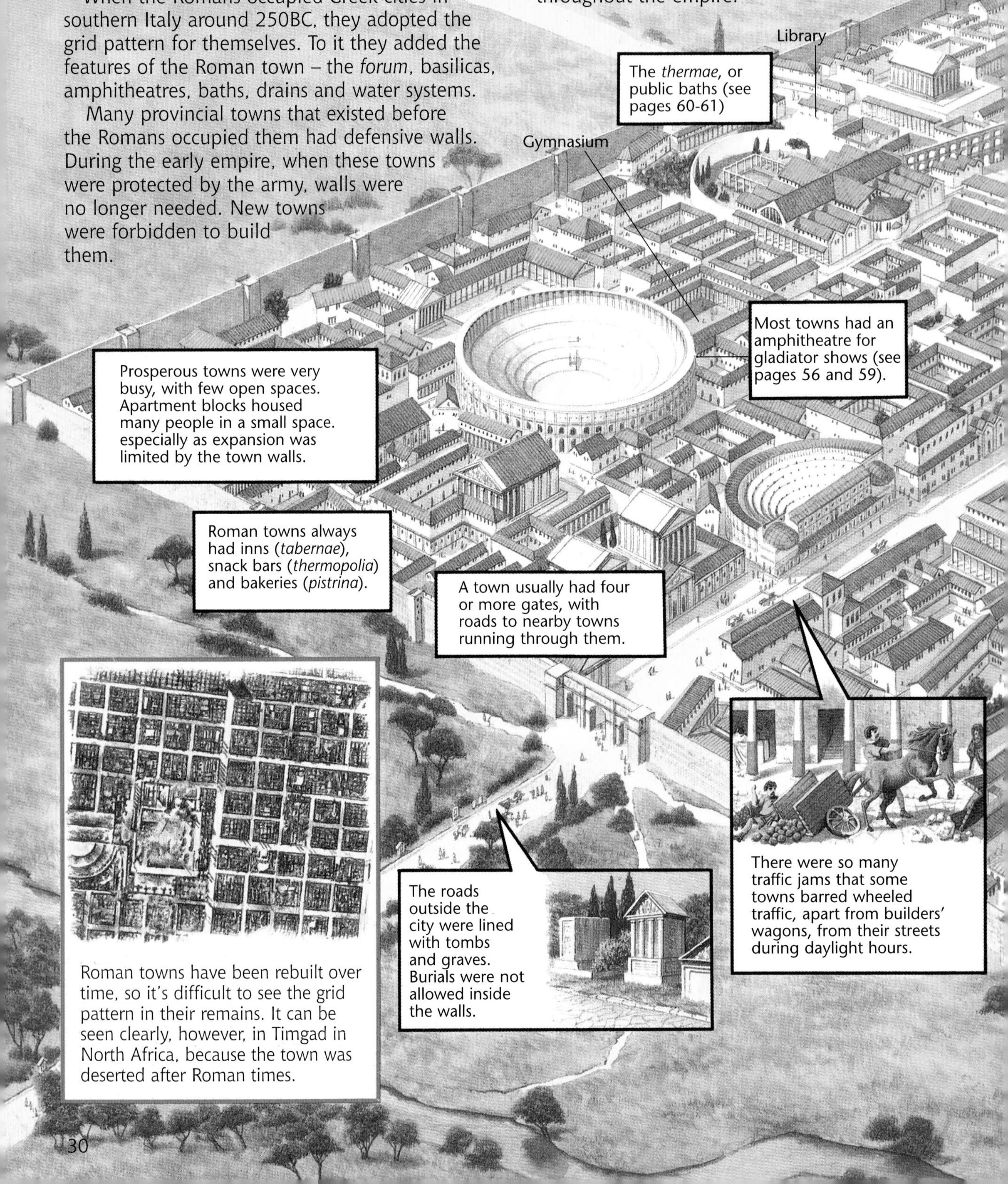

Library
The *thermae*, or public baths (see pages 60-61)
Gymnasium
Most towns had an amphitheatre for gladiator shows (see pages 56 and 59).
Prosperous towns were very busy, with few open spaces. Apartment blocks housed many people in a small space. especially as expansion was limited by the town walls.
Roman towns always had inns (*tabernae*), snack bars (*thermopolia*) and bakeries (*pistrina*).
A town usually had four or more gates, with roads to nearby towns running through them.

Roman towns have been rebuilt over time, so it's difficult to see the grid pattern in their remains. It can be seen clearly, however, in Timgad in North Africa, because the town was deserted after Roman times.

The roads outside the city were lined with tombs and graves. Burials were not allowed inside the walls.

There were so many traffic jams that some towns barred wheeled traffic, apart from builders' wagons, from their streets during daylight hours.

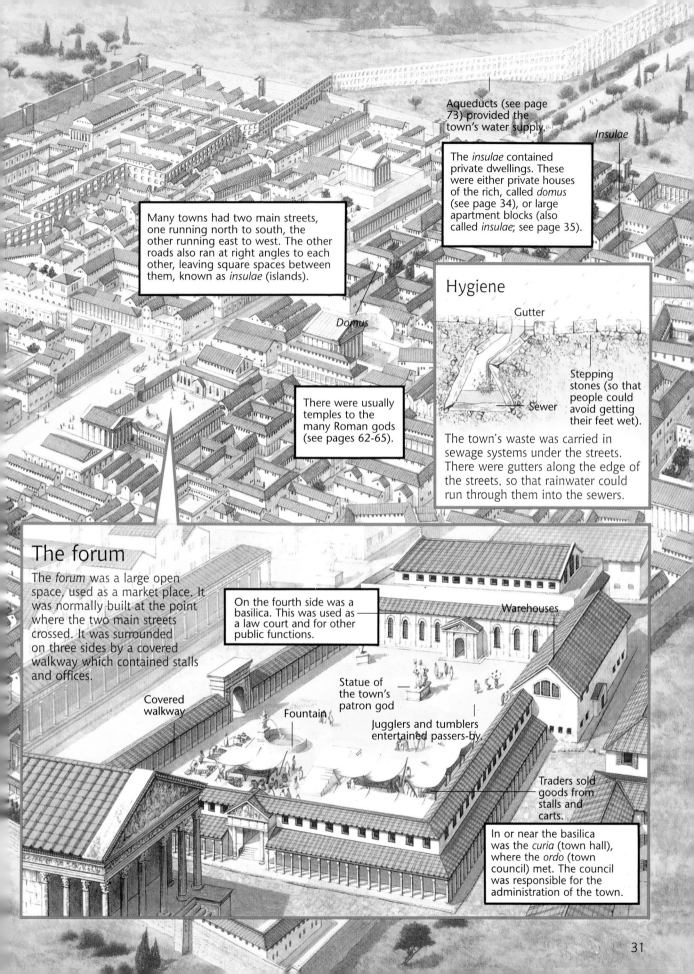

Aqueducts (see page 73) provided the town's water supply.

Insulae

The *insulae* contained private dwellings. These were either private houses of the rich, called *domus* (see page 34), or large apartment blocks (also called *insulae*; see page 35).

Many towns had two main streets, one running north to south, the other running east to west. The other roads also ran at right angles to each other, leaving square spaces between them, known as *insulae* (islands).

Domus

There were usually temples to the many Roman gods (see pages 62-65).

Hygiene

Gutter

Stepping stones (so that people could avoid getting their feet wet).

Sewer

The town's waste was carried in sewage systems under the streets. There were gutters along the edge of the streets, so that rainwater could run through them into the sewers.

The forum

The *forum* was a large open space, used as a market place. It was normally built at the point where the two main streets crossed. It was surrounded on three sides by a covered walkway which contained stalls and offices.

On the fourth side was a basilica. This was used as a law court and for other public functions.

Warehouses

Covered walkway

Fountain

Statue of the town's patron god

Jugglers and tumblers entertained passers-by.

Traders sold goods from stalls and carts.

In or near the basilica was the *curia* (town hall), where the *ordo* (town council) met. The council was responsible for the administration of the town.

31

The city of Rome

From a small hilltop settlement, Rome grew into the largest, most magnificent city in the ancient world. The empire's wealth and power was reflected in the capital city's public buildings and monuments.

Emperors commissioned new buildings to compete in size and luxury with earlier ones. But Rome was also overcrowded, with many squalid tenements. At its largest the ancient city had well over a million inhabitants. This is a reconstruction of Rome as it might have looked in imperial times.

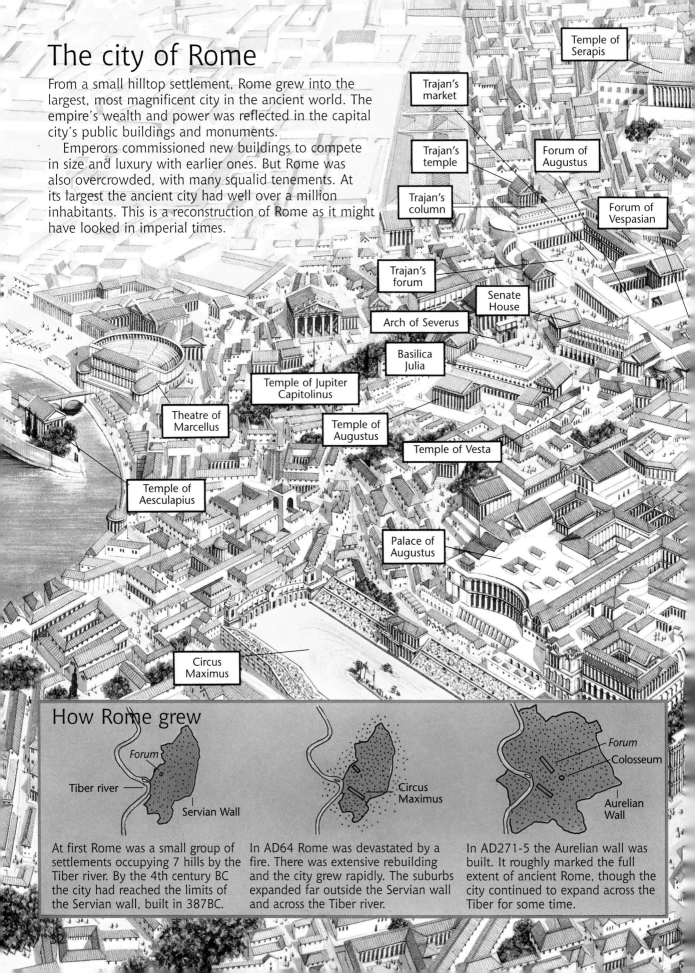

Temple of Serapis

Trajan's market

Trajan's temple

Forum of Augustus

Trajan's column

Forum of Vespasian

Trajan's forum

Senate House

Arch of Severus

Basilica Julia

Temple of Jupiter Capitolinus

Theatre of Marcellus

Temple of Augustus

Temple of Vesta

Temple of Aesculapius

Palace of Augustus

Circus Maximus

How Rome grew

Forum

Tiber river

Servian Wall

Circus Maximus

Forum

Colosseum

Aurelian Wall

At first Rome was a small group of settlements occupying 7 hills by the Tiber river. By the 4th century BC the city had reached the limits of the Servian wall, built in 387BC.

In AD64 Rome was devastated by a fire. There was extensive rebuilding and the city grew rapidly. The suburbs expanded far outside the Servian wall and across the Tiber river.

In AD271-5 the Aurelian wall was built. It roughly marked the full extent of ancient Rome, though the city continued to expand across the Tiber for some time.

Baths of Constantine

Basilicas, like the one shown above, were huge public buildings used as law courts and offices. After the rise of Christianity (see page 65) many basilicas were turned into churches.

After the fire in AD64 Nero built a palace called the Golden House, and put this statue of himself in the grounds. The palace was torn down when he was deposed, and the statue's head was replaced with that of the god Apollo.

Basilica of Maxentius

Temple of Venus and Rome

Statue of Apollo

Colosseum

Baths of Trajan

Temple of Jupiter Stator

Arch of Constantine

Ludus Magnus

Aqueduct of Nero

Temple of the Divine Claudius

Triumphal arches, like the arch of Constantine (above) were built to celebrate battle victories. There were several arches in Rome, and many similar ones in the provinces.

The Temple of the Divine Claudius was built in AD54, when Claudius was declared a god. There were temples all over the city dedicated to the many Roman deities.

Town houses

By the time of the later republic, most townspeople lived in apartment blocks known as *insulae*. Each apartment was known as a *cenaculum*.

Only the very rich could afford a private house, or *domus*. A survey of Rome in AD350 listed 1,790 *domus* and 46,602 *insulae*.

A domus

Most town houses had the same basic plan. Some, like this one, had a second floor, but this wasn't very common.

Guests were received in the *atrium*. The word comes from the word *ater*, meaning black. In early times the *atrium* was the only room, and it was blackened by smoke from the fire.

The rooms at the front opened on to the street. They were often rented out to traders.

The roof sloped down to an opening called the *compluvium*. It could be covered in canvas in cold weather.

Rain collected in a shallow pool called the *impluvium*. When the water rose to a certain level, it was piped to a tank under the house.

The family lived in the rooms at the back of the house between the *atrium* and the garden.

Tablinum (study)

Windows were left open, or covered with wooden shutters, animal skin or layers of semi-transparent stone. Glass windows were rare.

A walled garden like this was called a *peristylium*.

The *lararium*, a shrine to the household gods, was kept in the garden or in the *atrium*.

Kitchen (see page 40)

The dining room was called a *triclinium* (see pages 38-39).

Most houses had no bathrooms, because in every town there were many public bath-houses (see pages 60-61).

Central heating

The Romans developed their heating system, known as the hypocaust, in the first century AD.

When a house was being built, fire grates were built in the basement. The floor at ground level was supported by concrete or brick pillars. Fires were lit in the grates. Warm air circulated under the floors and through ducts in the walls. The pillars retained their heat for a long time.

We don't know how the Romans adjusted the heat, apart from building up the fire or damping it down.

Floor

Fire grate

Pillars

Insulae

Some apartments were luxurious, while others were cramped and squalid. Limits were imposed on the height to which *insulae* could be built – four or five floors were usually allowed.

Poorer tenants lived in the upper floors, which were built of wood. The rooms were small and often in very bad condition. Some landlords built extra rooms so they could make more money, but these were often badly constructed. This made buildings very unsafe, and many collapsed.

Woodburning braziers were the only form of heating used, but these were a great fire risk and there were no chimneys.

The *insulae* had no internal drains, so people threw their waste into gutters in the streets.

Rich occupants often had several well-furnished, comfortable rooms to live in.

Few *insulae* had their own toilets. People had to use public lavatories like this.

Cooking was impossible in the flats, so people ate cold snacks, or went to inns and bars for their meals.

The lower floors, usually built of stone, were for richer tenants.

There was no running water, but people fetched water from the many public fountains nearby.

The rooms at street level were sometimes let as shops or taverns. People rarely lived in the ground-floor rooms of *insulae*.

The floors were connected by a staircase.

Firefighting

Fire was a constant risk in Rome, because of the hot, dry climate, the overcrowded conditions, and the use of open fires in wooden buildings. Augustus set up a fire service for Rome. There were seven brigades, called *vigiles*, each with 1,000 men. The city was divided into 14 regions and each brigade was responsible for two of them. These fire brigades were copied in other towns, though on a smaller scale.

Simple hand-held pumps were used for small fires.

Undamaged walls were dampened to stop the fire spreading.

Furniture

Roman houses were sparsely furnished. Many rooms were too small to hold much furniture. Most surviving Roman furniture is made of marble or metal, but wood may have been more common.

Cushions and mattresses were filled with wool or feathers.

Beds

Beds and couches were used in studies and dining rooms as well as bedrooms, in place of sofas. Luxurious bed-frames were made using precious metals.

A blanket was the only covering.

Some other kinds of Roman beds

Chairs

Scamnun

Folding chair

Sella

Bisellium

A Roman stool was called a *scamnum*. Stools with four legs were often made of bronze, instead of wood.

The *bisellium* was used by wealthy or important people, while the *sella* was more common in homes.

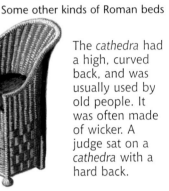

The *cathedra* had a high, curved back, and was usually used by old people. It was often made of wicker. A judge sat on a *cathedra* with a hard back.

Tables

Tables varied in price, and Romans were prepared to spend large sums of money on them. As the Romans frequently ate outside, marble or stone tables were common.

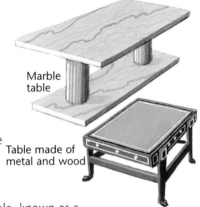
Marble table

Table made of metal and wood

The one-legged table, known as a *monopodium*, was particularly expensive. The central support could be carved in ivory, or made of elaborately cast metal. Precious, rare woods were sometimes used for the tops.

Storage

For storage, the Romans used heavy chests and cupboards.

Heating & lighting

The Romans used oil and taper lamps to light their houses. For heating they used small bronze braziers, or enclosed heaters which looked more like modern stoves. For fuel they used wood, charcoal, or coke, a refined form of coal.

A brazier

Oil lamps were made of terracotta or metal. They burned vegetable oil (from olives, nuts or sesame) or fish oil. Thousands of oil lamps have survived.

The wick protruded through a nozzle at the front.

Lamps were long and flat, with a handle at the back.

There were also hanging lamps with chains and hooks.

Lanterns were widely used. The flame was protected by pieces of horn, or animal bladder. Later lanterns were made of glass.

Decorations

The Romans were more interested in how houses looked inside than how they appeared from the outside. While many town houses looked drab from the street, their interiors were lavishly decorated with wall paintings and mosaics.

At first the styles and techniques were adopted from the Greeks. Many Romans employed Greeks to decorate their rooms, because they were thought to be the best artists. This reconstruction shows decorators at work in a Roman house.

Artists began painting pictures on the walls while the plaster was still damp. Paintings done in this way are called frescoes.

Paintings of the countryside and nature were popular.

Architectural scenes were also common.

Paints were made from ground rocks, plant extracts or animal dyes.

Figures from Greek mythology were often depicted.

Walls were also painted with portraits, possibly of the owner of the house.

Mosaics (pictures made of small pieces of tile or stone) were popular in Rome by the 1st century BC.

Wet plaster was spread over a small area, then stones were pressed into it.

Different stones were used to make patterns like the one shown here.

Companies of mosaicists designed the mosaic away from the house. Then someone came to the house with a plan, and the stones already cut.

Statues

Rooms were decorated with brightly painted statues, but the paint has now worn off.

Sea creatures were built into fountains.

Gods and goddesses, and animals were common subjects.

Food and dining

For breakfast most Romans ate bread or wheat biscuits with honey, dates or olives. The *prandium* (lunch) was a similar meal, but instead of eating lunch, many Romans waited until the main meal of the day, the *cena*, in the afternoon.

During the early republic, the *cena* was very simple. The most common food was wheat, often eaten as a kind of porridge with sauces and vegetables. Later, however, for the wealthy, meals became more elaborate.

A dinner party

In rich imperial households, the *cena* was often very lavish. Hosts displayed their wealth by giving luxurious meals for their friends or for important people. During the republic, only men attended formal dinners, but by imperial times, women often dined with the men. In early Rome people sat on chairs. Later, people dined lying on couches.

Romans did not use knives and forks. They mostly ate with their fingers, or sometimes with spoons.

Slaves wiped the guests' hands between courses.

Poets performed at more elegant banquets.

The fourth side of the table was left clear for slaves to bring food to the table and remove empty dishes.

The slaves also served wine with the meal. Sometimes it was heated in a warmer.

The menu

The dinner came in three courses. The first consisted of such appetizers as salad, radishes, mushrooms, oysters and other shellfish, sardines and eggs. This course was followed by a drink of *mulsum* (wine sweetened with honey).

The main course contained as many as seven dishes, including fish, meat and poultry. These were served with vegetables and sauces.

Rather than clearing the dishes after the main meal, the slaves removed the table and replaced it with another one with fruit, nuts and honey cakes. This part of the meal was known as the *secundae mensae* (second tables).

Food was served with plenty of wine. The Romans had over two hundred varieties from various parts of the empire. The best was said to come from Campania, near Naples.

Roman recipes

A recipe book from the fourth century AD, written by a food expert named Apicius, gives us details of some Roman dishes and how they were cooked.

Sauces were made with great care. The most common, called *liquamen* or *garum*, was made from fish, salt and herbs. It was so popular that it could be bought ready-made. *Defrutum*, another sauce, was made by boiling fruit.

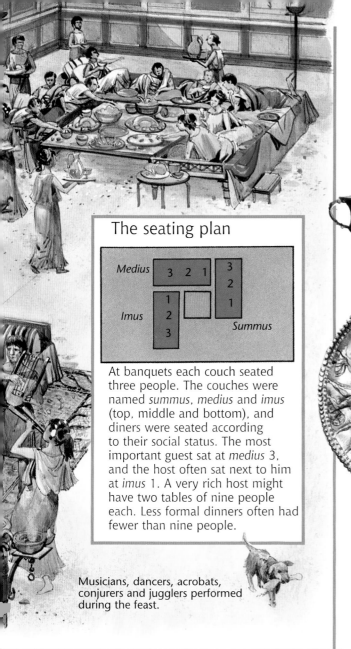

Dining utensils

Food was served on dishes. Most were made of glass or pottery, but if the host was very rich there would also be ornate platters of gold and silver. Some examples are shown below.

Glass was often extremely ornate.

Silver drinking cup

Spoons

Silver strainer

Red pottery like this was popular all over the empire. It is known as Samian ware.

The Romans were highly skilled metalworkers. Rich households often had intricately decorated dishes like this.

The seating plan

Medius

	3	2	1		3
					2
	1				1
Imus	2				
	3				

Summus

At banquets each couch seated three people. The couches were named *summus*, *medius* and *imus* (top, middle and bottom), and diners were seated according to their social status. The most important guest sat at *medius* 3, and the host often sat next to him at *imus* 1. A very rich host might have two tables of nine people each. Less formal dinners often had fewer than nine people.

Musicians, dancers, acrobats, conjurers and jugglers performed during the feast.

Music and musicians

Though some rich citizens learned to play musical instruments they always remained amateurs, because they thought it was undignified to play, sing or dance in public. Professional musicians and dancers were usually slaves or freed men. As well as performing at dinner parties they also played in processions and parades, in the theatre and at the games. Here are some of the instruments they played.

Pipes   Lyre   Flute   Tambourine

Cymbals

Stuffed dates

For dessert Romans often ate stuffed dates. You can make these yourself.

Mash together some chopped apple and nuts, bread or cake crumbs, a pinch of cinnamon or nutmeg, and a little fruit juice.

Chop the tops off the dates and remove the stones.

Push the filling in with a spoon.

In the kitchen

Most simple houses or apartments had no kitchens. The occupants could not cook in their living rooms because of the fire risk, so they had to visit the tavern for a hot meal. But rich people had large, well-equipped kitchens in their houses.

Kitchens were staffed by slaves, who spent most of the day preparing the main meal. Food was cooked in earthenware or bronze pots on a stove of hot charcoal.

Pots like this, with pointed bottoms, called *amphorae*, were used for storing wine or oil.

Small *amphorae* were laid on shelves.

Meat and poultry was roasted on spits over fires.

Large *amphorae* were propped up in the corner.

The cooks had sharp knives to chop vegetables.

For sauces, ingredients were ground with a pounder called a pestle, in a stone bowl called a mortar.

Kitchen utensils

Unlike the elaborate glass and metal utensils used for serving meals (see page 39), cooking pots were simply and strongly constructed to withstand a lot of use.

Jugs had very thick sides and a small opening, perhaps to keep water cool in hot weather.

This pottery strainer may have been used to drain liquid from curd cheese.

Some pans could be used for cooking or serving. This one also had a close-fitting lid.

Knives were beaten or cast out of metal, then sharpened.

Metal sieves were used for straining wine or sauces.

Cooking pots were often placed on stands so that they did not rest directly on the fire.

This Roman relief shows slaves at work in a kitchen.

Two slaves are stoking the furnace.

A third is scooping flour from a sack.

Another is making dough or pastry.

Jewels and ornaments

At the beginning of the republic jewels were rare. The law allowed only the upper classes to wear gold rings. Ornaments became more common, however, after the Romans gained territories in the east, where precious metals were readily available. The materials used were gold, silver, bronze and iron, set with precious and semi-precious stones.

Gem stones included opals, emeralds, sapphires and pearls. The Romans also polished glass and used it in place of precious stones. Both men and women wore rings. Women also wore a variety of earrings, necklaces, anklets, hairpins and brooches. Roman jewels have been found all over the Roman world. Here are some examples.

Gems often had designs cut into the surface, like this one found at Herculaneum.

Others were set into rings made from several pieces of gold.

A gold bracelet shaped like a snake was said to bring the wearer long life. These were found at Pompeii.

Fine gold chains were common. They were often made of many strands of metal.

This bracelet is made from many strands of fine gold wire.

Each leaf in this necklace from Pompeii was stamped out of a sheet of gold.

Pearl earrings like this were common around Pompeii and Herculaneum.

Earrings were mostly made of gold. This pair, set with emeralds, was probably made around Naples.

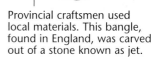

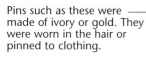

Pins such as these were made of ivory or gold. They were worn in the hair or pinned to clothing.

Provincial craftsmen used local materials. This bangle, found in England, was carved out of a stone known as jet.

Cameos

Minature carvings in semi-precious stone, known as cameos, were also popular. They were made from sardonyx, a rock with dark and light layers. Cameos were often worn as brooches or medallions.

The stone was carefully chosen to make sure that the different layers would contrast after it was carved.

Then the carver cut the design into the top layer, leaving the underneath layer as a background.

The most popular designs were pictures of the imperial eagle, or portraits of famous people.

This skeleton, found at Herculaneum, shows that Romans might have worn rings between the first and second joints of the finger, as well as below the second joint.

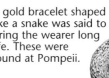

Clothes and fashion

Fashions in Rome changed very little for nearly a thousand years. Most people wore clothes made from wool or linen. In imperial times fine cotton cloth was imported from India, but was very expensive. Silk, from China, cost three times its weight in gold. Fur and felt were also used, especially in colder climates.

Most garments were made from large uncut pieces of cloth which were folded and pinned with pins known as *fibulae*, or tied with belts. Garments needing a lot of sewing were rare, as most needles were made of bone and therefore very clumsy. Clothes were mainly undyed, but some were bleached white or dyed various shades.

Men's clothes

A man's only underwear was a loincloth. He probably slept in one as well. Over this he wore a tunic, made from two rectangles stitched at the sides and shoulders, and tied with a belt. Augustus is said to have worn four tunics at once when the weather was cold.

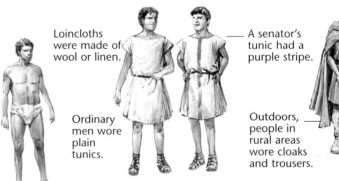

Loincloths were made of wool or linen.

Ordinary men wore plain tunics.

A senator's tunic had a purple stripe.

Outdoors, people in rural areas wore cloaks and trousers.

The toga

Originally only citizens could wear the *toga*. Worn over the tunic, at first it was just a large wool blanket wrapped around the body. Later it became more elaborate with complicated folds. Many people disliked the *toga* because it was heavy and awkward, and hard to keep clean. But emperors tried to keep it in use because it was so distinctive. Senators' *togas* were decorated with a purple stripe.

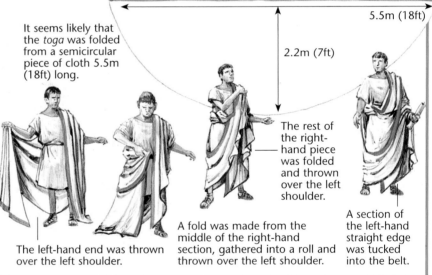

It seems likely that the *toga* was folded from a semicircular piece of cloth 5.5m (18ft) long.

5.5m (18ft)

2.2m (7ft)

The rest of the right-hand piece was folded and thrown over the left shoulder.

The left-hand end was thrown over the left shoulder.

A fold was made from the middle of the right-hand section, gathered into a roll and thrown over the left shoulder.

A section of the left-hand straight edge was tucked into the belt.

Women's clothes

As underwear women wore a loincloth and, sometimes, a bra or corsets. Over this went a tunic, probably of fine wool or linen. On top of this was worn the *stola*, a robe which reached the ankles.

In early times women wore the *toga*, but later the *palla* was fashionable. It was a large piece of cloth which could be draped over the *stola* in many ways.

Tunic

Many women wore a veil or scarf to protect their hair.

Some women wore the *palla* over their heads.

Palla

Stola

Tunics were often made of plain, undyed cloth.

Children's clothes

Most children wore tunics like those of their parents. Some boys wore the *toga praetexta*, a garment with a purple stripe. At about the age of 14 a ceremony took place and they began to wear adult clothes (see page 48).

This mosaic shows children in tunics.

Toga praetexta

Bulla

Some young girls wore the *stola*.

Men's hairstyles

During the early republic, many men wore beards, but it later became the fashion in Rome to be clean-shaven. Most Roman men wore their hair short, but during imperial times some fashion-conscious men had longer hair which was oiled and curled. Some popular hairstyles are shown here.

Republican hairstyle

Later hairstyle

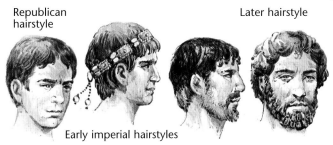

Early imperial hairstyles

The barber's shop was a place to meet friends and gossip. Being shaved was painful. Although the razor was sharp the barber used no oil or soap, so cuts and scars were frequent.

Women's hairstyles

Rich women spent a lot of time and money on their hairstyles, and had slaves to do their hair for them. Some popular styles are shown here.

During the republic most women wore a simple bun.

In imperial times hairstyles were ornately braided and curled.

Makeup

Women used various substances as makeup. They stored these in small pots and bottles.

Women whitened their faces with powdered chalk.

Hairpins

To tint their lips and cheeks red, they used the sediment from red wine, or a plant dye called *fucus*.

Heated tongs were used to curl hair.

Makeup pot

Hair comb

Shoes

During the early republic, many Romans went barefoot most of the time. Outside they wore leather sandals. Later, footwear became more elaborate, and shoemakers became skilled at creating ornate footwear out of canvas and leather.

Leather sandals

Soldiers often wore boots that had soles studded with nails.

Women wore elegant sandals like these.

Outside, men wore heavy boots, or *calcei*.

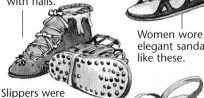

Slippers were made of soft leather or cloth.

The Roman villa

The Romans used the word *villa* for a country house. Wealthy Romans saw the countryside as a source of income and as a place to rest from city life. Many villas were owned by rich city-dwellers who only spent part of the year in the country.

At other times the estate was run by a manager and slaves. Most villas were also farms. A few were supported by industries such as pottery or mining. A small number were lavish palaces that existed simply for their owners' pleasure.

An Italian villa

Most of the villas that have been excavated date from late imperial times. Few earlier villas remain as they were often rebuilt at a later stage.

This reconstruction is based on remains found at various Italian sites. It shows a villa on an estate that made its money from farming and wine making.

Decorations

Villas were often lavishly decorated, with mosaics (see page 37) on floors and walls. This mosaic showing musicians is from a villa near Pompeii.

Triclinium (dining room)

Kitchen

The part where the owners lived was very luxurious. It was known as the *villa urbana*.

Paintings

The walls were painted with murals. Countryside scenes like this one were very popular.

A villa in the provinces

When the Romans conquered northern Europe, the area consisted mostly of peasant farmers who lived in simple huts. The conquest opened up new opportunities for many of them and a new class of natives emerged – wealthy landowners who adopted Roman customs. They built large farmhouses based on Roman ones. The pictures below show how this new style of farmhouse developed.

One of the wings had two floors.

Before the conquest (c.AD50) the farmhouse was round with a thatched roof.

Around AD60, after the Roman conquest, it was rebuilt as a rectangular hut.

About ten years later it was rebuilt and enlarged, with five rooms and a verandah.

Around the end of the 2nd century a new style of villa, known as a winged-corridor villa, emerged. The verandah was replaced by a corridor with a wing at each end. Later, in some villas, the wings were extended and linked with a wall, forming a courtyard inside.

The baths may have been used by both the owners and the workers.

Room where grapes were pressed

There was a large area of farmland where vegetables were grown for the staff to eat.

Cow shed

This part of the villa, called the *villa rusticana*, was used by the farm staff.

Grape juice was fermented to make wine.

The granary floor was raised on bricks to prevent damp reaching the grain.

Hadrian's villa

Hadrian had a magnificent villa at Tivoli, northeast of Rome. Its many buildings included a stadium and baths. The gardens (shown here) occupied around 18 square km (7 square miles), and featured pools and an island.

Ornaments

The gardens were decorated with fountains, and statues of gods, people or animals. This statue of a child holding a fish formed the spout of a fountain.

Late provincial villas

By late in the 3rd century AD, villas in Britain were more lavish. Much of Europe was under attack from barbarians and rich citizens from dangerous provinces may have sought refuge in Britain. This is a reconstruction of a 3rd-century villa at Chedworth, Gloucestershire.

The courtyard alone was bigger than the manor house that was later built there.

The foundations were built of chalk and flint.

The lower parts of the walls were made of flint and mortar.

Farming

Farming was one of the Romans' most important industries. Although basic farming methods changed little over the centuries, the Romans developed ways of making farms more efficient and productive. They introduced these ideas all over the empire and took better equipment to primitive countries like Britain. They also spread new crops through the empire.

During the early republic most farms were very small. These farmers grew enough to live on, and sold any surplus.

During the Punic wars many farms were neglected, as farmers had to join the army.

Many farmers couldn't afford to repair their farms. Rich landowners bought their land and turned it into large farms.

An imperial farm

Many imperial farms produced a variety of goods, but some concentrated on one or two products. This farm has been reconstructed from paintings, reliefs and mosaics, some of which are shown in the inset boxes.

Farmers kept as many as 200 chickens for their eggs and meat. Ducks and geese were also kept.

The ground had to be turned over before seeds were planted. Seed was sown in autumn, and again in spring if needed.

Pigeons were kept in dovecotes and used as food in winter.

Grape press

Honey was the only form of sweetening available to the Romans, so they kept bees.

Lettuce   Carrots

Radishes

Cabbages

Beans

Many farms were dedicated to growing food for the inhabitants of nearby towns.

The most important working animal was the ox. The ones in this relief are pushing a threshing machine.

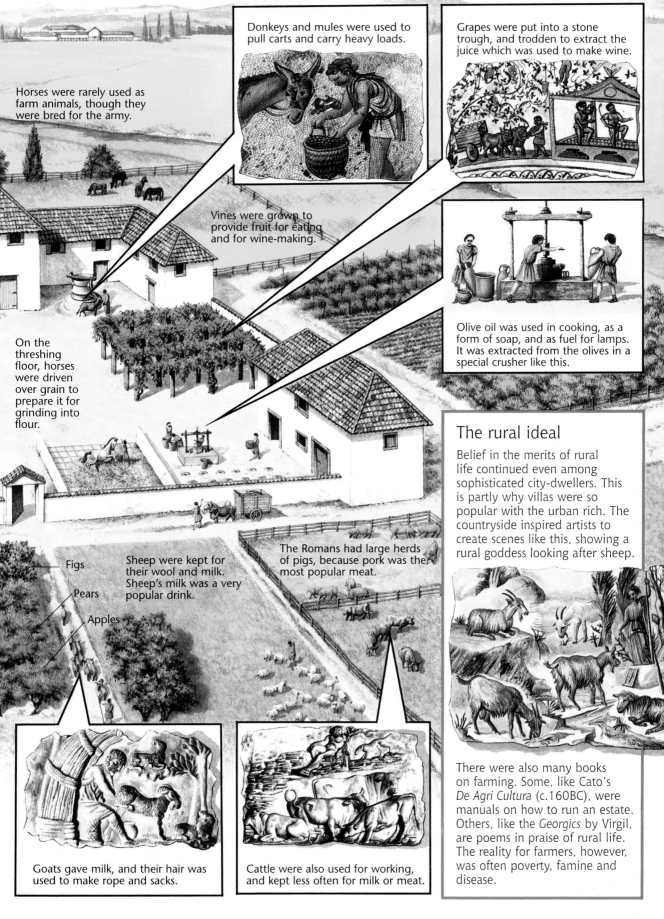

Donkeys and mules were used to pull carts and carry heavy loads.

Grapes were put into a stone trough, and trodden to extract the juice which was used to make wine.

Horses were rarely used as farm animals, though they were bred for the army.

Vines were grown to provide fruit for eating and for wine-making.

On the threshing floor, horses were driven over grain to prepare it for grinding into flour.

Olive oil was used in cooking, as a form of soap, and as fuel for lamps. It was extracted from the olives in a special crusher like this.

The rural ideal

Belief in the merits of rural life continued even among sophisticated city-dwellers. This is partly why villas were so popular with the urban rich. The countryside inspired artists to create scenes like this, showing a rural goddess looking after sheep.

Figs

Pears

Apples

Sheep were kept for their wool and milk. Sheep's milk was a very popular drink.

The Romans had large herds of pigs, because pork was the most popular meat.

Goats gave milk, and their hair was used to make rope and sacks.

Cattle were also used for working, and kept less often for milk or meat.

There were also many books on farming. Some, like Cato's *De Agri Cultura* (c.160BC), were manuals on how to run an estate. Others, like the *Georgics* by Virgil, are poems in praise of rural life. The reality for farmers, however, was often poverty, famine and disease.

Marriage and childbirth

Parents chose husbands and wives for their children and often arranged marriages for political, business or social reasons. Girls could marry at the age of 12, but most waited until they were at least 14. There were different types of marriage contracts. In republican times a woman's money and possessions could become the property of her husband's father.

Later, women controlled their own belongings and had more freedom.

The wedding day had to be carefully chosen because many days in the Roman calendar were thought to be unlucky. Weddings often took place in the second half of June, which was considered a particularly lucky period.

To celebrate an engagement, a party was held and the marriage contract was written out. The bride was given a ring. The night before the wedding, she offered her childhood toys to the household gods.

On the wedding day, the bride wore a white tunic, a headdress of flowers, and a red veil and red shoes.

The priest asked the gods if the day was lucky. If it was, then the ceremony continued.

The contract was signed and the bridesmaid joined the couple's hands. The bride vowed to follow her husband wherever he went.

A party was held at the house of the bride's father. Then the bride and groom led a procession of guests, flute players and torchbearers to the groom's house. The groom carried the bride over the threshold.

Childbirth

Childbirth was very dangerous in Roman times. Medical science was primitive, and we know from tombstones that women often died giving birth. Children often died when they were still very small.

Women married early partly because they believed that childbirth was safer when they were young. Some richer women, after giving birth to an heir, avoided having more children by using sponges as contraceptives.

On the ninth day after the birth a naming ceremony took place. The child was given a *bulla*, a charm to ward off evil spirits.

A new baby was bathed and picked up by its father. This showed that it had been accepted into the family.

Becoming an adult

When a boy was about 14 years old, usually after he had finished his basic education, a ceremony was held at which he formally became an adult. With family and friends he went to the *forum*, where he discarded his childhood clothes and *bulla*. He was given an adult's *toga* and his first shave, and was registered as a citizen. A party was held to celebrate.

48

Funerals

Funerals were based on the Romans' beliefs about what happened after death. People thought a dead person's spirit was rowed across a mythical river (the Styx) to the underworld (Hades). The spirit was judged, then went to heaven (Elysium) or hell (Tartarus). Funerals prepared the spirit for the journey. A coin was placed under his or her tongue to pay the ferry fare to Hades.

At the funeral of a very important person, the body was placed on a portable bed known as a litter. This was carried to the *forum* as part of a procession.

The body lay in state in the *atrium*.

When a nobleman died his body was washed and covered in oil.

If the man held political office he was dressed in his official robes. Otherwise he wore a *toga*.

People came to pay their respects.

Praeficae (professional mourners) followed the corpse.

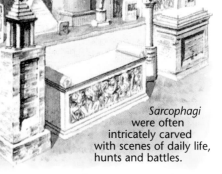

Musicians

At the *forum*, a speech was made in praise of the dead person.

In republican times relatives rode in front wearing death masks and mourning robes. This had stopped by imperial times.

Burial

By law graves had to be outside the city. Main roads were lined with tombs. The body was placed in a coffin called a *sarcophagus*.

Sometimes, instead of burying the body, the Romans cremated it. In simple ceremonies they dug a pit, filled it with wood, and burned the body. They covered the ashes with earth.

In more elaborate rituals the body was burned on a ceremonial fire called a pyre. Clothes and food were thrown in, in case the dead person needed them later.

Sarcophagi were often intricately carved with scenes of daily life, hunts and battles.

Sometimes pillars or even high towers were built to mark graves. This one at Igel in Germany is 23m (75ft) high.

When the flames of the fire had died down, they were doused with wine.

The ashes were collected and placed in a jar called an urn. Urns were sometimes placed in an underground chamber known as a *columbarium*.

Education

Many poorer children never went to school as they needed to work. Rich children attended a *ludus* (elementary school) when they were about six.

Most children left at the age of 11, and had any further education at home. But girls often began to prepare for marriage at this age.

The school day

Most schools only had one room, on the ground floor of a house or behind a shop. There was usually only one class, of about 12 children. Teachers were often Greek slaves. The Romans respected the knowledge and learning of the Greeks. Remains of pupils' exercises, and descriptions by Roman writers of their education, tell us about the school day.

Older children had to learn and recite the works of famous authors.

Young children recited the alphabet and learned to read and write.

Rich families employed a slave called a *paedagogus* to take the children to school and supervise them in class.

Some pupils wrote on wooden tablets coated with wax.

Some pupils scratched their writing on bits of pottery.

The grammaticus

Around the age of 11 some boys went to a teacher known as a *grammaticus*, who taught such subjects as history, philosophy, geography, music and astronomy. One of the most important subjects was Greek, because Greek culture had such a big influence on Roman life. Works of Greek and Roman literature were studied in great detail. Greek was also necessary for Romans because most of the best books on other subjects were written by Greeks in the Greek language.

Pupils were expected to be able to imitate the styles of famous authors.

Further education

The job of the *grammaticus* was to prepare the student for study with a teacher of public speaking, known as a *rhetor*. Anyone who wanted to be a politician or lawyer had to learn to speak in public. This training began when a youth was 13 or 14, and could take many years; Cicero, a famous speaker, continued his studies until he was nearly 30. Only the wealthiest people could afford to give their children this education, so few poor people became politicians or lawyers.

The *rhetor* taught his pupils how to write and present speeches properly.

Rhetor

Writing

Pupils wrote by scratching on panels of wood coated with wax, using a metal pen called a *stylus*. When the tablet was used up, the wax was scraped off and more was applied. Some children wrote on pieces of broken pottery. Older pupils used pens made from reeds or metal. They wrote on sheets of papyrus (see below) with ink made of gum and soot.

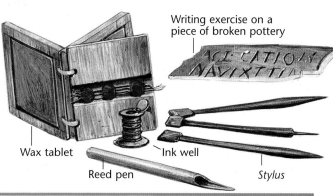

Writing exercise on a piece of broken pottery

Wax tablet

Reed pen

Ink well

Stylus

Papyrus

In Roman times paper made from wood pulp hadn't been invented. Instead, a material made from an Egyptian reed called papyrus was used.

The Roman method of making papyrus paper, and joining it into scrolls, is shown in the pictures below.

A sheet was formed of two layers of strips, placed at right angles to each other and pressed together.

The outer rind of the reed was removed and the core was cut into long, narrow strips and soaked.

The sheet was beaten with a mallet, left to dry, and polished with a stone.

The sheets were glued together to form a longer one. When this was dry it was rolled into a scroll.

Wood or ivory rollers were put at each end to make it easier to handle.

The joins between the sheets could hardly be seen in well-made scrolls.

Books

The Romans were very fond of books. In large cities like Rome and Alexandria there were numerous bookshops and publishers. Many people treasured books, and built up large collections of them. Libraries were even set up for public use.

By the late Empire there were 29 libraries in Rome. Books took a long time to make, because each one had to be written out by hand. They were copied by scribes who were often Greek slaves. This picture shows how a manuscript was copied.

Publishers employed a man to read the book to a team of scribes. Each scribe wrote a copy of the book.

The text was written in columns. When one column was finished the scribe began another one to the right.

Rolls varied in length, but were commonly around 10m (30ft). Many were beautifully illustrated. Some had parchment covers.

The rolls were often stored in a leather casket.

The codex

In the 4th century AD the scroll began to be replaced by the *codex* or book. The *codex* was soon adopted by the Christian Church because it held more information than a scroll, and was easier to store, carry and read.

Jobs and occupations

Upper-class Romans did not respect physical work, and would consider only a few careers, such as the army, politics, or some forms of financial work. Skilled jobs like architecture (see pages 70-73) or medicine (see pages 68-69) were done by educated members of the middle class, foreigners, or freed men (see opposite). Most poorer citizens worked as craftsmen or shopkeepers; those in rural areas owned or worked on farms (see pages 46-47). Manual work like building or mining was done almost entirely by slaves (see opposite).

Most craftsmen worked in small workshops at the back of houses, selling their goods at the front. Others bought their goods from wholesale markets and then sold them to the public. A Roman street might have contained some of these stalls.

Meat from specially bred cattle was sold wholesale to butchers at a market known as the *forum boarium*. The butcher then sold to the public. Some butchers sold poultry as well.

Carpenters made furniture or worked in the building trade. The workshop was equipped with many types of tools still in use today.

Potters designed and made crockery of all kinds. They cast pots on wheels and baked them in kilns over wood fires.

Bakers ground flour and baked bread, then sold it over a counter to the public. The loaves had distinctive patterns.

Metalworkers made tools, weapons, and household goods out of bronze, iron and copper, as well as brooches, rings and ornaments out of gold, silver and jewels (see page 41).

Working women

The lives of Roman women depended on how rich they were. Rich families thought it inappropriate for women to go out to work.

Wealthy women were expected to have babies and organize the running of the home. Slaves helped them bring up their children.

In ordinary families women had to spin and weave wool cloth to make clothes. All women were taught these skills, but most rich families bought ready-made cloth.

Poorer women worked in markets, as needlewomen, or as attendants at the baths. Some served customers, as shown in this relief.

In the country, women worked on farms and as shepherdesses. A farmer's wife worked on the land with her husband.

Slaves and slavery

Slaves were workers with no rights who were owned by Roman citizens, or by the state. They were bought and sold like any other property, and their lives were controlled by their owners.

There were few slaves during the early republic, but after the 3rd century BC the number grew as Rome conquered other countries. After each new victory prisoners of war were brought back to Rome.

Slaves were sold by auction to the highest bidder.

A slave's life

In imperial times there was a vast workforce of slaves. Their lives varied depending on the jobs they did and whom they worked for. Many slaves suffered terribly at the hands of cruel masters, but others lived well. Here are some of the jobs that slaves did.

Greek slaves were thought to be the cleverest. They worked in richer Roman houses as doctors, tutors, artists and librarians.

Other slaves worked as hairdressers, butlers, maids and cooks. Some helped their owners in workshops or factories.

Slaves owned by good masters in the country often lived better than poor citizens in towns. They worked in pleasant surroundings, and could marry and have children. Many also ran small farms of their own.

The government owned many slaves, who maintained buildings, bridges and aqueducts. Others worked as civil servants, helping the administration of the empire. Some became very powerful and important.

Slaves who worked in mines suffered particularly bad conditions. They were harshly treated and forced to work constantly in mines that were often unsafe. Many died as a result of injuries or beating.

There were several rebellions by discontented slaves. The most famous was led by Spartacus, who formed a huge army of slaves in 73BC. It was defeated by the Roman army two years later.

Some slaves were paid wages. If they saved enough money, they could pay their masters to set them free. Others didn't have to pay, as some owners freed slaves who had served well.

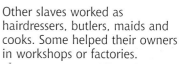

At the freedom ceremony the slave wore a special cap and was given a *toga praetexta*.

By imperial times freed slaves were a large, rich group. Many owned businesses. Others became important administrators or civil servants (see page 27).

Money and trade

In the early republic money was not used; people simply exchanged one kind of goods for another (known as bartering). Later, people used blocks of bronze weighing one Roman pound (327g/11.44oz).

As the Romans gained territory, they became richer and the economy became more complex. By imperial times an intricate economic system coordinated money and trade all over the empire.

Republican coins

Coins were first used by the Greeks. After seeing Greek coins in central Italy, the Romans opened their first mint around 290BC. Soon there were several mints, all producing their own coins.

The first Roman coin, the *as*, was bronze.

Around 269BC the first silver coin, the *didrachm*, was introduced.

Later, the silver *denarius* was issued. This one shows a man voting in the elections.

There were at first 10, and later 16 asses to a *denarius*.

Another silver coin, the *sestertius*, was first worth 2.5 asses, later 4.

The *aureus* was Rome's first gold coin.

Coins were used to mark important events. 'EID MAR' on this one means 'The Ides of March', the date of Caesar's assassination.

Early imperial coins

When Augustus became emperor he took control of the mints, and supervised the making of all gold and silver coins. But mints in the provinces could make their own bronze and copper coins.

These were less valuable than coins made of gold and silver. Augustus gave all coins a fixed value. They were used all over the empire, and this encouraged trade (see opposite).

Every coin had the emperor's head on it to prove it was genuine. The largest gold coin was still called the *aureus*.

This is a silver *denarius*. An *aureus* was worth 25 *denarii*.

The *sestertius* was minted in bronze, not silver; there were 4 *sestertii* in a *denarius*.

A *dupondius* was worth half a *sestertius*.

The *as* was made of copper. There were 4 to a *sestertius*.

There were 2 bronze *semis* to an *as*.

There were 4 copper *quadrans* in an *as*.

Later imperial coins

Prices rose constantly, so people could buy less and less with their coins. New ones of higher values had to be minted. But the cost of precious metals increased too, so mints had to reduce the weight of coins, or make them in copper with only a thin coating of precious metal.

This type of coin, known as a *solidus*, was issued by Constantine. He intended it to become the standard coin, as it was difficult to forge and everyone knew what it was worth. The *solidus* was made from about 5g (0.16oz) of gold.

By the end of the Empire period, people became suspicious of money because prices rose so quickly and forgeries were common. Many Romans abandoned coins and returned to bartering.

Banking

After the Punic wars, the Romans controlled a huge trading network. Merchants needed money for trading, so banking and moneylending became important parts of the economy. These services were run mainly by *equites* and freed salves, as patricians thought financial work was undignified. Members of the middle classes became very rich.

This relief shows a banker at his desk. There were bankers all over the empire. Some were run by the state, but others operated individually.

When people found themselves unable to repay their debts they had their property confiscated. Some were even sold into slavery.

Taxes

The government imposed taxes to raise money to run the state. Taxation changed from time to time, and differed in each area. Some of the main types of taxes are described below.

Provincials, and later Roman citizens themselves, paid tax on their property, houses, farms, slaves and animals. Inspectors assessed how much tax people had to pay.

Transactions such as buying and selling property or slaves were subject to tax. People also paid tax on money they inherited. This relief shows people paying a tax collector.

There was no organized system of distributing food to soldiers. Instead farmers had to reserve a portion of their grain and other goods for troops based on their land.

Trade

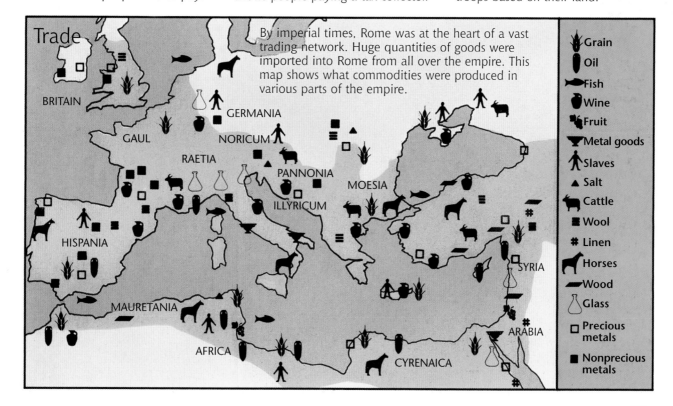

By imperial times, Rome was at the heart of a vast trading network. Huge quantities of goods were imported into Rome from all over the empire. This map shows what commodities were produced in various parts of the empire.

BRITAIN
GERMANIA
GAUL
NORICUM
RAETIA
PANNONIA
MOESIA
ILLYRICUM
HISPANIA
SYRIA
ARABIA
MAURETANIA
AFRICA
CYRENAICA

Grain
Oil
Fish
Wine
Fruit
Metal goods
Slaves
Salt
Cattle
Wool
Linen
Horses
Wood
Glass
Precious metals
Nonprecious metals

Entertainment

Many citizens had lots of free time, as slaves did most of their work. Evidence of leisure activities comes from archaeological finds, mosaics, paintings, and the writings of Roman authors. Some activities are described here and on the next five pages.

Pastimes

Public gardens and parks were popular places to relax and chat. Romans also enjoyed many forms of exercise, including running, javelin throwing and wrestling. There was also space for less energetic activities like the ones described below.

People used game boards, or scratched crisscross patterns on the ground.

Gambling games with coins included *capita et navia*, the Roman equivalent of heads and tails.

A game known as *tali* was played with pieces of bone or pottery. The pieces had numbers on the sides and were thrown like dice.

Rich men were fond of hunting and fishing.

We know from the writings of Horace that children built toy houses, used whips and tops, kites and hoops, and played on seesaws and swings. Reliefs, paintings and mosaics show pictures of the games children played.

Dolls were shaped out of clay, then carved and painted. Rag dolls and jointed dolls made of wood were also common.

Clay doll —

Wooden jointed doll

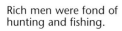

Sometimes children rode in carts pulled by geese, as shown in this mosaic.

The drama

Drama became popular during the 3rd century BC after the Romans came into contact with the Greeks. At first plays were staged in primitive wooden buildings, but in 55BC the first stone auditorium was built in Rome by Pompey. It held up to 27,000 people, and similar ones were later built all over the empire. Remains show us what things might have looked like on the inside.

Each part of the auditorium was reserved for a different class of people. The poorer they were, the higher up they sat.

In early days, the public stood to watch the play. Later auditoriums had stone seats.

People brought cushions to make the seats more comfortable.

People could leave quickly at the end of the play, because there was an intricate network of corridors and stairs.

To keep the sun off the spectators, canvas covers were spread over the auditorium, stretched from poles at the back of the top row of seats.

Roman actors wore masks on stage. This was because most Roman plays included the same types of characters, and the masks made them easier to identify from a distance.

Scenery was sometimes hung behind the actors.

The scenery was manipulated by complicated machinery.

Scene changes were hidden by a curtain which was lifted from a slot at the front of the stage.

The actors appeared on the *pulpitum* (stage).

At first only men were allowed on stage. Later, women performed too.

Benches were arranged in front of the stage with the best seats reserved for senators.

The audience was rowdy, clapping, booing, hissing and even fighting. Some actors were so popular that they were mobbed by their devoted fans.

Plays and writers

The first play was shown in Rome in 240BC. It was a Greek drama, translated into Latin by a Greek former slave named Livius Andronicus. Though serious plays were popular at first, audiences began to want comedies. The most famous Roman comic writers were Plautus and Terence. This painting shows a scene from a play by Plautus.

Gradually theatrical shows became more spectacular, to compete with races and public games (see pages 60-61). Eventually people went along more to see the special effects than the plays themselves.

57

Races and games

Public sports and shows in Rome were called *ludi* (games). There were three kinds: theatrical performances (*ludi scaenici*, see page 56), chariot races (*ludi circenses*), and gladiator fights and beast hunts (*munera*).

At first these public events were staged together to form an entire day's entertainment. By imperial times, however, each event could be seen as a separate entertainment, often in its own specially designed building.

Chariot races

Chariot racing was the most popular spectator sport in Rome. Races were held at a racetrack known as the circus or hippodrome. As many as 24 races took place in a day, with up to 12 chariots from four different teams. The races were directed by an important person (sometimes the emperor himself) who started each race by throwing a white cloth from his platform.

A central rib, the *spina*, ran down the middle of the course, with three pillars at each end.

Laps were counted by moving counters shaped like dolphins or large eggs on the *spina*.

There were four teams - red, green, blue and white.

The drivers jostled for a position close to the *spina*. This was to secure the shortest route around the bend.

The driver wound the reins around his body, and carried a knife to cut through them if he was thrown from the chariot.

The *Circus Maximus* in Rome was the largest and oldest racetrack in the empire. It was 550m (over 1,800ft) long and 180m (almost 600ft) wide, and held up to 250,000 spectators.

Usually either two or four horses pulled each chariot, but sometimes special races were held with six or even eight horses to a team. The more horses, the harder it was to control the chariot.

Each team had its own stables and trainers. Supporters were fanatical, and unpopular results could lead to riots. Champion drivers, like the one in this mosaic, became very rich and famous.

Gladiator fights

Gladiators were prisoners, criminals, slaves or paid volunteers. Fights and shows involving wild animals were popular in Rome. At first, like chariot races, they were held in the circus, but later they were staged in buildings called amphitheatres. Games were often put on to mark an important event like a battle victory. The earliest games were small, but they became more extravagant. Trajan presided over a show that lasted 117 days in which 10,000 gladiators took part.

There were amphitheatres all over the empire. The largest held up to 50,000 spectators.

Games began in the morning with a procession past the seat of the emperor or presiding official. The gladiators were accompanied by dancers, jugglers, priests and musicians.

Next came the beast shows. Some rare animals were simply displayed. Others, like bears, panthers and bulls were forced to fight each other, hunted in the arena by archers, or let loose on terrified prisoners. Many fights involved the violent killing of thousands of animals and humans. After the beasts came comic acts, mimes and mock fights.

Vats of incense were used to disguise the smell of blood.

Murmillo

Samnite

Thracian

Retiarius

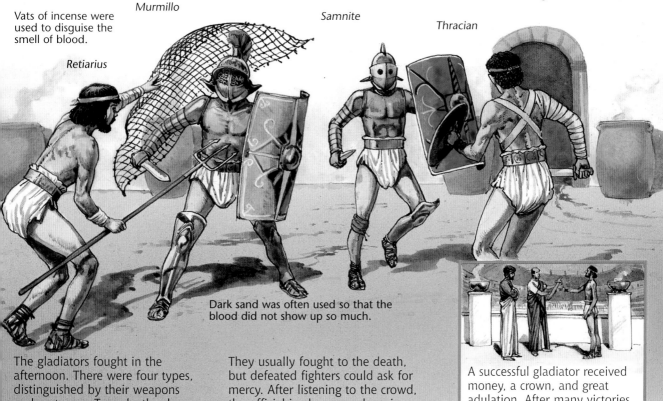

Dark sand was often used so that the blood did not show up so much.

The gladiators fought in the afternoon. There were four types, distinguished by their weapons and costumes. To make the show more interesting, gladiators in different categories fought each other; for example a *retiarius* might fight a *murmillo*.

They usually fought to the death, but defeated fighters could ask for mercy. After listening to the crowd, the official in charge made a sign with his thumb to show whether the man should live or die. The 'thumbs up' signal probably meant the man should live, but experts are not sure.

A successful gladiator received money, a crown, and great adulation. After many victories he might be awarded a wooden sword, which signified his freedom. Many freed fighters became trainers at special schools for gladiators.

The baths

The first bath-houses, built in the 2nd century BC, were simple washing facilities for men only. But by the time of Augustus there were 170 privately owned bath-houses, and in AD20 the first state-owned public baths opened. Baths grew in size and luxury in imperial times; they became popular meeting places where thousands of people spent their leisure hours.

Emperors had baths to show off their wealth and the buildings were often extremely lavish. We know from the ruins of baths that they were also sophisticated buildings with complicated heating and plumbing systems. This is what a Roman bath-house might have looked like.

There were several baths at different temperatures.

The *frigidarium* was a room with a large cold swimming pool.

Clothes left in the *apodyterium* (cloakroom) were often stolen.

There was an exercise yard for wrestling, training and various kinds of sports.

Rich people took their slaves to the baths to help them and look after the clothes.

Various snacks were sold for the bathers to eat.

Some baths also had stalls and restaurants, either in the complex itself or close by.

Baths were often built in places where the water was thought to have medicinal properties. People thought that the waters would cure their illnesses.

Sometimes there was an outdoor pool.

A huge wood-fired hypocaust system (see page 34) conducted heat under the floors and into the room.

The hottest room of all, the *laconicum*, was used mainly by invalids.

The *caldarium* (hot room), had a bathing pool. People sweated a lot in this damp atmosphere.

Libraries and reading rooms were common in the larger baths.

After bathing, customers could hire attendants for a massage. Barbers and hairdressers were also available, as were beauty treatments.

The *tepidarium* was a warm room with a small pool.

Keeping clean

The Romans did not have soap. To remove dirt and sweat they covered their bodies with oil which they scraped off with strigils (scrapers made of wood, bone or metal).

People played games of *tali* (see page 56), or dice.

Famous baths

Among the most impressive baths in Rome were those opened by the emperors Caracalla and Diocletian. This is a reconstruction of the Baths of Caracalla.

The gardens were a good place to socialize and catch up with all the latest gossip.

Religious beliefs

Roman gods and goddesses formed two groups: those that looked after the home, and those of the state religion, celebrated at public ceremonies.

Worship of household spirits was the earliest form of Roman religion; the rituals of the state religion became more elaborate as the empire grew.

Worship at home

Romans believed that their homes were controlled by groups of *numina* (household spirits). One group, the *penates*, protected goods and property; another, the *lares*, looked after the whole household. Every house had its own shrine to the lares called a *lararium*. Each family also had its own guardian spirit, the *genius*, and ancestral spirits, the *manes*. Some *numina* took on individual personalities and names. These included Vesta, goddess of the hearth, and Janus, god of the doorway.

The family prayed at the *lararium* each day and offered gifts of food and wine.

The growth of religion

As Roman territory grew, the Romans encountered people who believed in other gods and goddesses. Rather than suppressing these other religions, they often adopted them. As the empire expanded the number of deities increased.

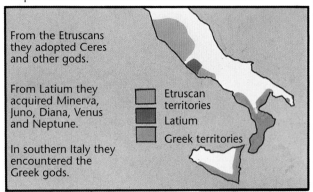

From the Etruscans they adopted Ceres and other gods.

From Latium they acquired Minerva, Juno, Diana, Venus and Neptune.

In southern Italy they encountered the Greek gods.

Etruscan territories

Latium

Greek territories

The state religion

The Romans were attracted to Greek mythology. They matched their gods with the Greek ones (see overleaf), making them the basis of the state religion. This involved performing strict rituals at elaborate ceremonies.

People believed that they were protected by a particular deity. They also believed that each god looked after a particular aspect of life. For example, Venus granted success in love, and Mars in war.

Temples and ceremonies

The state deities had large and impressive temples built for them. Their layout was adopted from those of the Etruscans and Greeks. Temples contained treasure that had been won in battle or had been donated by individuals as a way of thanking the god for help. People were also allowed to store their own gold in the temple, which was looked after by priests and priestesses.

The temple housed the statue of the god.

On public holidays and festivals (see pages 66-67) a procession of priests, officials and musicians led animals to the temple to be sacrificed.

Ceremonies were held outside the temple, but individuals could go inside for private prayer.

Making sacrifices

Animals were sacrificed at an altar in front of the temple. Only priests could conduct the ceremony. If any detail of the ritual went wrong, the Romans thought the gods would not accept the sacrifice. Priests were therefore very important. The chief priest was known as *Pontifex Maximus*. From the time of Augustus this position was held by the emperor.

Citizens brought beasts to the temple as offerings. The animals most frequently used were oxen, sheep, pigs, goats and doves.

The priest washed his hands, called for silence, and sprinkled salt, flour or wine on the animal's head. When he gave the signal, attendants carried out the sacrifice.

Parts of the animal's carcass were thrown onto the altar fire for the god to consume.

Foretelling the future

The Romans believed strongly in supernatural forces. They had many ways of predicting the future and learning the will of the gods. Some of these are shown below.

Haruspices were priests who studied the innards of sacrificed animals. It was thought that the shape of an animal's liver, and the presence or absence of blemishes on it, would reveal the gods' views about government projects and policies.

In Rome there was a group of 16 prophets known as augurs. They examined the sky for flocks of birds, cloud shapes, lightning, and other natural events. They believed that these things were omens that could reveal the opinions of the gods.

In times of national crisis, the Romans consulted books of prophecies written by the Sibyl, a prophetess who lived in caves in Cumae in early republican times. The books were closely guarded, and contained advice about how to interpret the will of the gods.

Astrologers told fortunes by examining the position of the stars at the time of a person's birth. By imperial times the practice was very widespread. Even emperors consulted astrologers, to protect themselves from assassination.

Poorer people had ways of foretelling the future, including palm reading and throwing dice.

People also thought that illness could be cured by miracles or by treatments suggested in dreams. To have such dreams the patient slept in the temple of Aesculapius, the god of medicine (see page 69).

Gods and goddesses

This family tree shows the main gods of the state religion (see page 62). The Greek name of each god is in brackets.

Uranus == Gaea

Cronus == Rhea

Vesta (Hestia), goddess of the hearth

Ceres (Demeter), goddess of agriculture

Juno (Hera), wife and sister of Jupiter, goddess of women == Jupiter (Zeus), king of the gods, and god of thunder and lightning

Neptune (Poseidon), god of the sea

Dis (Pluto), god of the underworld

Vulcan (Hephaestus), god of craftsmen and forges

Minerva (Athena), goddess of crafts and war

Mercury (Hermes), god of trade and thieves, Jupiter's messenger

Mars (Ares), god of war

Diana (Artemis), goddess of the moon and hunting

Bacchus (Dionysus), god of wine

Venus (Aphrodite), goddess of love and beauty

Apollo, god of the sun, music, healing and prophecy (The Romans adopted Apollo from the Greeks.)

== This symbol means 'married'.

The Vestal Virgins

Vesta, a state goddess, had a shrine in the *forum*, where a fire burned constantly. It was tended by six women called Vestal Virgins, who are shown in this relief. They were chosen from Rome's leading families. It was a privilege to be selected, but they had to do the job for 30 years and were not allowed to marry.

Other deities

There were many lesser gods. Some, like Flora and Faunus, were gods of growth and fertility. There were several gods of war, including Quirinus. The god of love was Cupid, and Roma was the goddess of Rome.

Flora

Cupid

Quirinus

Roma

Alternatives to the state religion

Many Romans lost faith in the state religion, as it offered little more than rituals. Also, when affairs of state went badly people found it increasingly hard to believe that sacrifices and prayers had any effect. By the start of the Empire many Romans had abandoned the state religion.

Augustus tried to restore it, but people wanted other religious experiences and turned to various cults that reached Rome from other places. These required people to take part in ceremonies rather than just watch them. Here are some of the gods, goddesses and religions that the Romans adopted.

Epona

Epona

Epona was the Celtic goddess of horses. Her cult was spread, probably by soldiers from Gaul, to Spain, Germany, the Danube, Scotland and into Italy itself.

Mithras

Mithras

Worship of the god Mithras began in India and Persia. Mithraism became popular all over the Roman world. It offered life after death, and asked people to treat others with kindness. The religion stated that all men were equally worthy, whether senators or slaves, but women weren't allowed to join the cult.

Cybele

Cybele, an important foreign goddess, was also known as the Great Mother. She ruled fertility, healing and nature. Her cult was brought to Rome from Asia Minor in 204BC, when a prophet warned that the Romans would lose the Carthaginian wars without Cybele's help.

Cybele

Judaism

The Romans encountered Judaism when they conquered Palestine in 63BC. At first Judaism was tolerated, but later Jews were persecuted because they believed in only one god and refused to worship the emperor. There were many revolts against Roman rule, and in AD70 the Romans destroyed the Jewish temple at Jerusalem. This event is shown on the arch of Titus.

Isis

The cult of Isis began in Egypt and later spread all over the empire. Isis was the ruler of heaven and earth, and goddess of wheat and barley. The cult became fashionable when the Egyptian queen Cleopatra spent the year 45BC in Rome. Isis was associated with goodness and the purification of sin. Ceremonies were very elaborate and mysterious.

This early Christian wall-painting shows Jesus as a shepherd.

Christianity

Christianity was founded in Palestine by followers of Jesus of Nazareth (c.5BC-AD29) and spread rapidly. It was popular with the poor, who found comfort in its promise of everlasting life. Like Jews, Christians had only one god, and refused to worship state gods. This angered the government, and Christians were persecuted. In AD313, official toleration of Christianity was declared. It became the official state religion in AD394.

Phoenician gods

Baal and Tanit were ancient Phoenician gods that the Romans encountered in Carthage. The rituals of their cult included human sacrifices, but these were forbidden after the Romans conquered Carthage in 146BC.

A shrine to another Carthaginian god, Melkart, was founded in 1100BC at Cadiz in Spain. By 400BC the Romans had linked Melkart to the god Hercules (himself derived from the Greek god Heracles). The cult continued into the 5th century AD.

Baal

Local gods

When the Romans conquered new areas they took their gods with them. Locals were not forced to adopt Roman gods, but they were often curious about them. Native deities merged with Roman ones, so local versions of state gods emerged all over the empire.

This temple in Germany was built for Mars Lenus, a god of healing.

65

Festivals

The Romans had many festivals, each with its own social or religious significance. They were often public holidays, although business was forbidden on only the most solemn occasions. During the rule of Augustus there were at least 115 holidays each year.

Under some later emperors there were more than 200 festival days a year. Many festivals were celebrated with games and theatrical performances (see pages 56-59). Below is a calendar of some of the most important events. Where known, the festival's Latin name is given.

January 1

New consuls were sworn in. They sacrificed bulls to Jupiter as thanks for his protection in the past year. The consuls promised that their successors would do the same the following year.

Early January: Compitalia

In the countryside, each farmer built a shrine with an altar. He placed a doll on it for each person in his household. The next day was a holiday. A sacrifice was made to purify the farm for the coming year.

In the city, the president of each *insula* sacrificed a hen on an altar built at each crossroads. Three days of celebrations followed.

February 13-21: Parentalia

The ceremony of *Parentalia* paid respect to dead parents. Romans visited cemeteries outside the city and placed flowers, milk and wine on the graves of their parents. This was to stop the dead from feeling hungry and returning to haunt the living.

February 15: Lupercalia

Two teams of youths met at Lupercal, a cave on the Palatine, and raced around the hill. Crowds gathered to watch. The runners dressed in the skins of sacrificed goats and were smeared with blood. As they ran they whipped the spectators with strips of goatskin. This was said to promote fertility, so women wanting children stood close to the race.

February 22: Caristia

This was a ceremony to conclude the Parentalia. It was an occasion on which families gathered together for a joyful dinner.

March 1

A ritual took place in the temple of Vesta at which the perpetual fire was rekindled. This day was also the beginning of the dances of the *Salii* (college of priests). Twelve young patricians danced around Rome holding sacred shields. This continued for 19 days.

March 14

Horse races were held in the *Campus Martius* to mark the feast of Mars, the god of war.

March 15

People had picnics by the River Tiber to celebrate Anna Perenna, goddess of the year. Some felt they would live as many years as they could drink cups of wine.

March 23: Tubilustrium

On this day sacred trumpets of war were purified at a ceremony to the god Mars. This was to bring success in the battle season.

April 4-10: Ludi Megalenses

Games were held to celebrate Cybele, the Great Mother (see page 65).

April 12-19: Ludi Ceriales

Games were held to celebrate Ceres, goddess of corn.

April 21: Parilia

Parilia began as a country festival to purify sheep and keep disease from the flock. But later it was celebrated in Rome because the date was said to have been the birth of the city. Festivities included bonfires onto which offerings were thrown. People danced in the flames. *Parilia* ended with a large outdoor feast.

April 28-May 3: Ludi Florales

This was a carnival for Flora, the goddess of flowers, and a celebration of fertility. It was also known as *Floralia*. People danced wearing brightly decorated garlands. Tables were piled high with flowers.

June 9: Vestalia

Married women went to the temple of Vesta with gifts of food for the goddess. *Vestalia* was a holiday for bakers, because the Vestal Virgins produced loaves made from *mola salsa*, a salted flour.

June 24: Fors Fortuna

This was the festival for the goddess Fortuna. There was a great public holiday. People rowed down the Tiber River to watch sacrifices at the two shrines to Fortuna, just outside Rome. The rest of the day was spent picnicking and drinking.

July 6-13: Ludi Apollinares

During the republic this festival was connected with religious ceremonies to the god Apollo. But by imperial times it was simply an excuse for theatrical shows, games and races.

August 12

The god Mercury was known for his sly practices and cunning. He was particularly popular among businessmen and traders, who paid 10% of their profits to his shrine. The money was used to pay for a public feast which took place on this day.

August 13

This day was a feast to Diana. Slaves had a holiday. It was also traditional for women to wash their hair.

September 5-19: Ludi Romani

At first this 15-day festival of games and plays was for Jupiter, but later much of the religious significance disappeared. On September 13 a cow was sacrificed at Jupiter's temple, and the Senate and all the magistrates ate a banquet. Statues of Jupiter, Juno and Minerva were dressed up and placed on couches so that they could share in the feast.

November 4-7: Ludi Plebeii

Drama, games and races marked this feast to Jupiter. On November 13 there was a banquet for senators and magistrates.

Early December: Rites of the Bona Dea

This festival celebrated Bona Dea ('Good Goddess'), whom the Romans believed protected women. The rituals were secret, and men were strictly forbidden to attend. The rites may have involved dancing, drinking and the worship of sacred objects.

December 17: Saturnalia

At first *Saturnalia* lasted only one day, but it was later extended to as many as seven. Pigs were sacrificed at the temple of Saturn and eaten the next day at a dinner where masters waited on their slaves.

Medicine

The Romans gained most of their knowledge of medicine from the Greeks. Hippocrates, a Greek doctor who lived in the 5th century BC, described all the illnesses he encountered and recorded how he treated them. His writings formed the basis of Greek and then Roman medical teaching. During the republic medical schools opened in Rome. Doctors had to learn many skills, for medicial methods often combined scientific treatments and religious rituals. Some doctors trained in army hospitals. They learned about anatomy and surgery from the wounds of soldiers. This is what a hospital tent might have looked like.

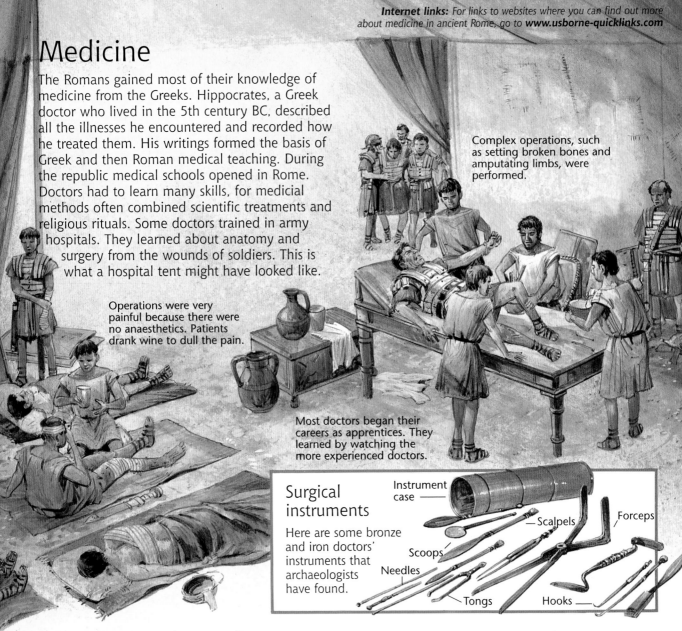

Complex operations, such as setting broken bones and amputating limbs, were performed.

Operations were very painful because there were no anaesthetics. Patients drank wine to dull the pain.

Most doctors began their careers as apprentices. They learned by watching the more experienced doctors.

Surgical instruments

Here are some bronze and iron doctors' instruments that archaeologists have found.

Instrument case

Scalpels

Forceps

Scoops

Needles

Tongs

Hooks

Treatments and remedies

Roman doctors knew that people's health was affected by what they ate. They also knew the benefits of exercise, fresh air and regular visits to the baths. Doctors used medicines made from plants, minerals and animal substances.

The remains of medicines have been found. It is hard to tell what they were made of and what they were used for, but we know about some of them because many documents about medicine have survived.

Eye infections were treated with ointments made with lead, zinc or iron.

The sap of certain plants was used to cure skin problems and snake bites.

Pill box

Medicinal herbs were added to wine. The mixture was drunk to cure coughs and chest complaints.

Ingredients were sometimes ground with a pestle in a mortar, then made into pills.

A visit to the doctor

Rich Romans had personal physicians to take care of them. Other wealthy patients paid doctors to visit them at home, but ordinary people had to go to a hospital or visit the doctor. In the 1st century AD a sort of state health service began. Each town had a number of doctors who were exempt from tax. They could accept fees, but had to treat the poor free of charge. Some doctors saw patients in rooms open to the street. Others had quieter rooms like the one shown here.

Cabinet with scrolls containing medical writings

Garden for growing herbs used to make medicine

Examination couch

Boxes containing medicines and ointments

Surgical instruments

Writers on medicine advised the doctor how to behave so as to make the patient feel at ease.

Other doctors

Archaeological evidence like this tombstone suggests that there were female doctors. They may have been midwives, assisting women in childbirth.

Some doctors went from town to town, treating people at each place they came to. They probably carried medicines with them to sell to their patients.

Dental treatment was also available. Technicians riveted extracted teeth to gold bridges to form false teeth. This was probably invented by the Etruscans.

Religion and medicine

The Romans linked religion and medicine because they believed that their deities could heal people. To obtain cures, many Romans performed religious rituals, while others relied on superstition and spells. Some doctors used these treatments as they too held these beliefs.

Throughout the Roman world there were temples to Aesculapius, the god of medicine. They contained statues of the god, like the one on the right. People slept in shrines, believing that their dreams would tell them how to cure their illnesses.

If they were cured, people gave offerings to the gods. Some showed the deities themselves. The one on the right shows Aesculapius and his daughter Hygieia, the goddess of healing.

There was a temple to Aesculapius on an island in the River Tiber. Slaves who were too old or ill to work were often left there. Claudius granted them freedom. Later the temple became one of the first public hospitals.

Architecture

In architecture, as in other areas, the Romans were influenced by the Greeks. They borrowed Greek styles, architects and craftsmen. But the Romans were quick to adapt and develop Greek ideas.

Their skills lay in the construction of huge buildings – amphitheatres, baths, basilicas, bridges and aqueducts. The introduction of concrete enabled them to build bigger, stronger structures than before.

Temples

The Romans copied Greek temple architecture very closely. Greek temples were mostly built in open spaces and could be seen from all sides. Roman temples, however, were often constructed in the middle of towns, surrounded by tall buildings, and only visible from the front.

The picture below shows the Maison Carrée, a Roman temple, built in the first century AD at Nîmes, France.

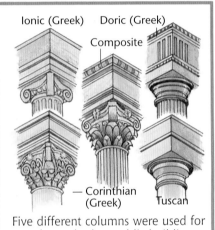

Five different columns were used for temples and other public buildings. They were based on Greek models.

Ionic (Greek) Doric (Greek)

Composite

Corinthian (Greek) Tuscan

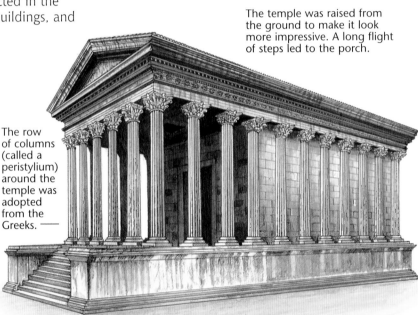

The temple was raised from the ground to make it look more impressive. A long flight of steps led to the porch.

The row of columns (called a peristylium) around the temple was adopted from the Greeks.

Arches

Before the Romans, most buildings were constructed with walls and columns topped by beams of wood or stone (known as trabeated architecture).

The Romans used these methods too, but they also developed the arch and the vault. The arch enabled builders to span greater distances. The method of building an arch is shown here.

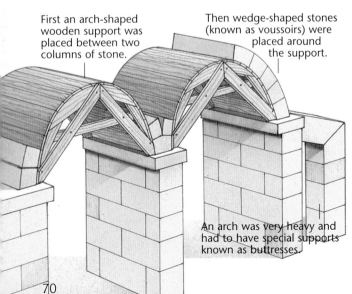

First an arch-shaped wooden support was placed between two columns of stone.

Then wedge-shaped stones (known as voussoirs) were placed around the support.

An arch was very heavy and had to have special supports known as buttresses.

The development of the arch enabled the Romans to build fine bridges and aqueducts such as the Pont du Gard in France.

In the Colosseum in Rome, shown here as it looks today, arches support the structure. The columns outside were only for decoration.

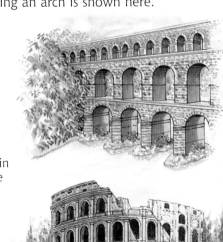

Vaults and domes

The Romans realized that a line
of arches side by side could
produce a tunnel vault to
enclose large areas. But this
allowed very little light
to enter a building.

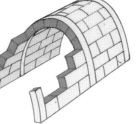

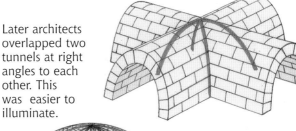

Later architects
overlapped two
tunnels at right
angles to each
other. This
was easier to
illuminate.

The groin vault was
first used at the baths
in Rome. On the left is
the *tepidarium* (warm
room) at the Baths of
Diocletian. Around
AD1550 this became
the church of Santa
Maria degli Angeli.

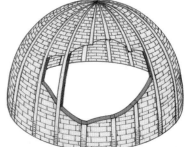

A further
development of
the arch was the
dome, made by
crossing a number
of different arches
over each other
to enclose a
circular area.

The Pantheon

Rome's Pantheon is the best example of a dome.
It was built in 25BC as a new form of temple by
Augustus's lieutenant Agrippa.

It's also a good example of the Roman use of
concrete. The Romans didn't know about reinforcing
concrete with metal so they had to
make it very thick to ensure
its safety.

The problem of illumination
was solved by leaving a
hole in the middle of
the roof.

The weight of the dome is
concentrated on a ring of voussoirs
which form the hole.

The dome is 43m (141.9ft)
high and 43m (141.9ft)
across. For many years, the
Pantheon was the world's
largest dome.

The outside of the dome
was covered with bricks
and strengthened by
frequent arches. Very
light concrete was used.

The inside was lightened
by recesses called coffers.

The exterior of the lower
part of the building was
coated with marble.

Building technology

We know that the Romans were highly skilled builders because so many of their constructions have survived into modern times. Their spectacular innovations in the fields of civil and mechanical engineering enabled them to construct vast, strong buildings and public works. Archaeological evidence tells us that the Romans chose the finest materials and devised many sophisticated construction methods to ensure that their buildings were safe and lasted many years.

This is how a Roman building site might have looked; the scene shows some of the methods, materials and equipment they used. Builders mostly used local supplies of wood and stone.

Interior walls in many houses were built from wooden frames filled with stones and cement. The finished wall was coated with plaster.

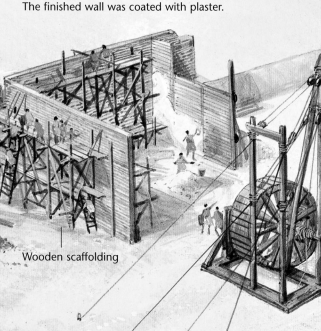

Wooden scaffolding

At first a soft volcanic rock called tufa was used, and later travertine, a fine stone from quarries near Rome.

Later builders began using marble from Italy and Greece.

Cranes, driven by slaves in a treadmill, made the lifting and positioning of heavy objects easier.

Concrete

The use of concrete was developed in the 2nd century BC. The Romans discovered how to make an excellent mortar out of volcanic ash, and so were able to build very strong structures. The stages of building a wall are shown here.

First two low brick walls were built with a space between them.

The space was filled with cement mortar and stones.

Once the concrete had dried, another wall could be built on top in the same way.

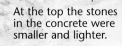

At the top the stones in the concrete were smaller and lighter.

Tiles and gutters were shaped out of clay and then baked to harden them. Every brick and tile had the name of the factory stamped on it.

Bricks were often laid in elaborate decorative patterns.

The Romans made excellent bricks, often rather flat and small. Bricklayers were highly skilled.

Civil engineering

Roads, bridges, buildings and water systems were all carefully planned. The Romans dealt very well with complex technical problems. Here you can see some Roman advances in civil engineering.

A good water supply was needed for public baths and lavatories. Water flowed into huge cisterns along aqueducts (pipes set into bridges or laid underground). It was then distributed through a complex system of pipes.

Water power was used to turn chains of water wheels. This is a reconstruction of a set of wheels in France which was used to drive flour mills.

Treadmills were used to get water from underground shafts. Water collected in troughs at the top of each wheel. Each trough was emptied by the wheel above.

Bridge building

First a temporary bridge was built over a row of boats. Wooden stakes, chained in circles, were driven into the river bed. The water was pumped out of this space.

Blocks of stone were placed inside the stakes, forming the pillars to support the bridge. When the pillars were tall enough, wooden frames were fixed between them. Arches were then built on top of the frames.

Tools and equipment

Roman metalworkers and carpenters made excellent tools for builders. Here are some examples.

The *groma* was used to estimate straight lines to make sure that buildings and roads were straight.

Stonemason's square

Cutting tool

Tongs

Trowel

Hatchet

The legal system

The first document to describe the Roman legal system in detail, known as the Twelve Tables, was published in 450BC. It was a list of rules and statutes, and covered many aspects of the law.

It contained laws about money, property, family and inheritance, and public order. The legal system changed over the years, but it was always based on the Twelve Tables during imperial times.

Courts and trials

Trials had to be set in motion by individuals, as the government itself did not prosecute people. Courts were managed in Rome by *praetores*, and in the provinces by governors. These men decided whether or not cases were worthy of trial, then chose the judge or tried the case themselves.

Anyone claiming that a crime had been committed had to summon the suspect to appear at court. People who did this gained great respect and prestige. In Rome, trials were held in basilicas near the *forum*. This is what a Roman court might have looked like.

Interesting or scandalous cases drew large audiences who often participated by shouting and jeering.

Trials took place in the rooms off the main hall.

In serious cases the accused paid a lawyer (known as an *advocatus*) to speak on his behalf. Good lawyers were highly respected.

If the suspect refused to attend the court the accuser could use force to take him.

In important cases a jury of up to 75 people was called.

Sometimes the accused wore rags, or brought his weeping wife and children to court, to make the jury feel sorry for him.

The jury decided whether or not the accused had committed the crime. The judge decided the punishment.

Crimes and punishments

Roman writings about law contain details of crimes and punishments. In imperial times the punishment depended on the status of the accused. Judges placed each defendant into one of two main categories: *honestiores* and *humiliores*. The *humiliores* were usually poorer than the *honestiores*, and got the worst punishments.

Many people were tried for crimes like not paying debts, not fulfilling contracts, or fraud. They had to pay fines or compensation.

Criminals were not imprisoned. Instead they were exiled to distant parts. Others lost their citizenship and had their property confiscated.

Laws and lawyers

The legal system based on the Twelve Tables grew into a vast code of laws and their interpretations. A ruling could be found to suit most circumstances. This diagram shows how the system worked.

Republican law

During the republic laws were made by the Senate and the Assemblies.

These laws were often imprecise, so judges had to decide how to apply them in court. This was part of a judge's skill.

When a judge took office, he issued an *edictum*. This listed his interpretation of each law, and was based on that of his predecessor.

Verdicts and judgements were written down and explained, so legal books not only listed the laws but also advised on how to interpret them.

Governors took local customs into account in the *edictum*, so laws differed in each province.

Imperial law

During the Empire the system changed. Most new laws were devised by the emperor.

Other laws, though issued by the Senate, still had to be approved by the emperor.

Judges still issued edicts interpreting the law, but their powers were reduced.

Later, Hadrian collected all the regional edicts and standardized them. A lawyer named Julianius Salvius was given the task of listing all the laws.

Augustus chose eminent lawyers to give their opinions on legal matters. In trials, judges had to follow these opinions and were not allowed to change or interpret individual laws.

Hadrian's reforms meant that all citizens had to obey the same laws. In AD212 citizenship was granted to free men throughout the empire. This meant that the law applied to all Roman people.

Roman citizens throughout the empire could appeal to the legal authorities in Rome if they thought they had been wrongly tried or sentenced.

The death penalty was rare during the republic. Crucifixion (death on a cross), flogging or beheading were common during the Empire.

Many *humiliores* who were sentenced to death either fought as gladiators or were savaged by wild animals in public games (see page 61).

Others were sent to be oarsmen on warships or to work in mines. Many prisoners died as a result of maltreatment and overwork.

The later Empire

After the rule of Marcus Aurelius (see page 25), political problems increased, caused by dishonest, brutal or incompetent emperors and rebellious soldiers. The Praetorian Guard became very powerful, often choosing or deposing emperors without consulting the Senate. This led to frequent changes of ruler, so the empire lacked the continuity and strong leadership it needed.

Commodus AD180-192; Pertinax AD192

Aurelius abandoned Nerva's method of choosing a successor (see page 25). He appointed his son Commodus, who made peace with the barbarians,

but then ruled irresponsibly. He was murdered in AD192. His successor, Pertinax, was killed after three months by the Praetorian Guard, who auctioned the throne. The winner was Didius Julianus.

Didius Julianus AD192; Septimius Severus AD193-211

Three army groups on the frontiers became jealous of the Praetorian Guard's power. They chose their own emperor, Septimius Severus, who returned to Rome and deposed Julianus. Severus kept the barbarians out for 14 years, but he raised taxes to pay the army. For the first time even Romans in Italy were taxed.

Caracalla AD211-217

Caracalla, Severus's son, raised the army's wages again, and paid barbarians to stay away from the borders. To increase the number of people he could tax, in AD212 he granted citizenship to all free males in the empire. He was murdered by his Praetorian Prefect, who seized power until he too was assassinated.

Bust of Caracalla

Elagabalus AD218-222

Elagabalus became emperor when he was 15. He was fanatically dedicated to worship of a Syrian sun-god. The Praetorian Guard killed him and chose his cousin Alexander as the new emperor.

Severus Alexander AD222-235

Alexander was only 13, so his mother Julia Mamaea ruled for him. She brought the army under control and improved social conditions. Teachers and scholars were subsidized, as were landlords who repaired their property. Julia achieved relative peace, but after 12 years the eastern frontiers of the empire were invaded. The army rebelled against the government and murdered Alexander and Julia.

The Anarchy AD235-284

Chaos followed. The throne went to an army leader, Maximinus Thrax, a barbarian who could hardly speak Latin and had never been to Rome. After this the empire was torn apart by civil wars. Various army factions nominated over 50 different rulers. Huge areas of the empire were ruined by famine, plague or invasion. Taxation was heavy and prices rose. Finally the wars ground to a halt, but the country was devastated.

Diocletian AD284-305

In AD284 Diocletian, a general in the Danube, was declared emperor by his troops. To establish order, he enlarged the army and made it responsible for running the empire. Aware of the threat posed by ambitious soldiers, he increased the number of generals but gave each one fewer troops. He split the provinces into smaller areas to make them easier to manage. More civil servants were appointed to handle the new administrative work.

Diocletian's most radical change was to divide the empire into two. Each half was ruled by its own Augustus and Caesar. Diocletian was Augustus of the East. In AD286 another soldier, Maximian, became Augustus of the West. This map shows how the empire was divided.

This statue represents the new system of leadership.

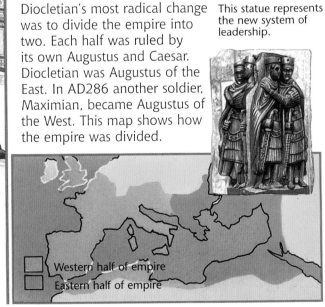

Western half of empire

Eastern half of empire

Diocletian's reforms

To stop prices from rising, Diocletian issued lists of the maximum sums that people could charge for goods and services. But this didn't work. In addition, the cost of defending the empire made it necessary to increase taxes. To make taxation more efficient, a census was taken every five years.

The law was enforced by the army which, as a result, became very influential.

Soldiers were now less able to depose the emperor, but they had more power over ordinary people. The Senate lost most of its authority, and in effect simply became the city council of Rome.

Diocletian declared himself a god and it was impossible for others to challenge him. In AD305 he resigned, persuading Maximian to do the same. He retired to a huge palace which was built for him at Spalatum in Dalmatia (now Split in Croatia).

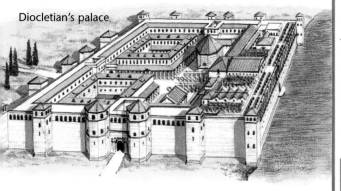

Diocletian's palace

Diocletian expected the two Caesars to take over, but this arrangement did not last long before the army interfered. By AD311 there were four contenders for the throne.

Constantine AD312-337

One contender, Constantine, was leading the army in Britain. In AD312 he returned to Rome with his troops and defeated Maxentius, his main rival, at the Milvian Bridge. It is said that before the battle Constantine saw a cross in the sky and the words *In hoc signo vinces* ('You will conquer with this sign'). After his victory he granted tolerance to all religious groups, including Christians (who under Diocletian had been badly persecuted).

Constantine adopted the Christian symbol shown on this tomb. It is made up of the first two letters of Christ's name in Greek: *chi* (χ) and *rho* (ρ).

Constantine's rule

Constantine began reuniting the empire. He defeated various rivals, and became the sole emperor in AD323. He granted freedom of worship to Christians and demanded to be treated as an earthly representative of the Christian God. He began taking part in religious discussions, and even became a Christian on his deathbed in AD337. In this way he cleverly transferred the ideas of the state religion – that the emperor had religious authority and divine status – to Christianity.

Constantine wanted a new capital city to rival Rome. In AD330 he moved his court to Byzantium, a former Greek colony, where he founded a new city called Constantinople (now Istanbul; see page 80). It remained an imperial capital for 1,000 years.

Under Constantine, the security of the empire depended on huge armies,

This head of Constantine, once part of a huge statue, was probably an object of worship.

and thousands of civil servants collected taxes. Workers were increasingly tied to their land and professions. But these measures failed to halt the decline of the economy.

Key dates

AD180-192 Commodus

AD192 Pertinax, Didius Julianus

AD193-211 Septimius Severus

AD211-217 Caracalla

AD218-222 Elagabalus

AD222-235 Severus Alexander

AD235-238 Maximinus Thrax

AD238-284 Civil wars.

AD284 Diocletian takes power.

AD286-305 Maximian rules western empire; Diocletian rules eastern empire.

AD293 Galerius and Constantius appointed Caesars; new system of government is formalized.

AD305-312 Struggles for power.

AD312-337 Constantine (East and West united again from 324).

The Empire after Constantine

After Constantine's death the empire was divided among his three sons, but struggles for power soon arose. After the death of two of them the third son, Constantius II, reunited the empire, but himself died in AD361.

His successor, Julian (AD361-363), was known as the Apostate (someone who abandons one religion for another). Julian restored the old Roman gods. Christianity wasn't banned, but people who followed the state religion were preferred. Julian was hardworking and conscientious. He cut the number of palace workers and gave back independence to city councils in the empire. His successor, Jovian (AD363-364), restored Christianity to its former supremacy.

Soon events outside the empire threatened its frontiers. The Huns, a tribe from eastern Asia, began moving west. They invaded the territory of other tribes, who in turn had to move west to escape them. In AD367 the Visigoths, Vandals and Ostrogoths set up their own kingdoms on Roman territory. This coincided with a series of short-lived emperors who were too weak to stop the invasions.

Julian

Barbarian soldiers

Theodosius was the last emperor to rule both East and West. In theory his sons were joint rulers of the empire, but they split it again and each ruled half. This scheme continued for another century; usually each emperor was succeeded by his eldest son. These rulers were often interested only in personal power and wealth. Meanwhile the barbarians continued to advance, further contributing to the downfall of the western half of the empire.

Honorius AD395-423

During Honorius's rule the barbarians shattered the security of the empire. In AD402 Italy was invaded by a tribe of Goths led by Alaric. Scared by this, Honorius moved the imperial court to Ravenna on the east coast of Italy. Gradually Ravenna grew from a poor town into a prosperous city. It remained an imperial city for centuries.

Ivory plaque showing Honorius

One of the oldest surviving buildings in Ravenna is known as the Baptistry of the Orthodox. It was built during the 5th century AD.

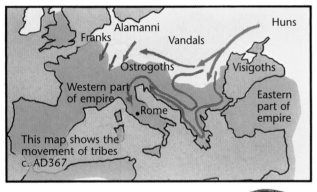

Franks
Alamanni
Vandals
Huns
Ostrogoths
Visigoths
Western part of empire
Rome
Eastern part of empire
This map shows the movement of tribes c. AD367

Theodosius AD379-395

During the unrest, Theodosius took power (AD379). He made a treaty with the barbarians from Germany. This granted them safety if they provided soldiers and farm-workers for the Romans. They became a regular part of the Roman army. Many Romans disliked this, but it was necessary as not enough Roman citizens were willing to become soldiers.

This silver relief shows Theodosius in his official robes.

While Honorous lived in luxury until his death in AD423, the empire was being overrun by barbarians. In AD409 the Vandals invaded Spain. In AD410 Rome was sacked by Alaric, who rapidly invaded the rest of Italy. That same year the Romans abandoned Britain and recalled the British legions to defend the shrinking empire. Disease and famine weakened the population. It is also likely that people stopped wanting to fight the barbarians, as they no longer had faith in the Roman government.

The barbarians take over

The barbarians swept across Europe. Part of Gaul was occupied by the Burgundians, and northern Europe by the Franks. In AD429 the Vandals moved from Spain to North Africa. In AD451 the Romans drove the army of Attila the Hun out of central France. But this was the last Roman victory.

The empire was continually under attack. In AD455 the Vandals destroyed Rome. Chaos and famine followed. Rome's population fell from over 1 million to about 20,000. Romulus Augustulus, the last emperor of the West, was deposed in AD476 by Odoacer, a German captain who declared himself King of Italy and ruled from Ravenna. The western empire had ended.

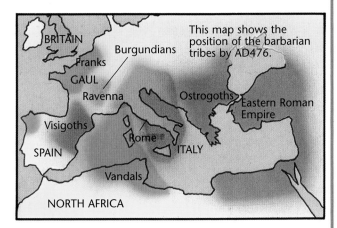

This map shows the position of the barbarian tribes by AD476.

BRITAIN
Franks
Burgundians
GAUL
Ravenna
Ostrogoths
Eastern Roman Empire
Visigoths
Rome
ITALY
SPAIN
Vandals
NORTH AFRICA

Barbarian rule

Many barbarians wanted to remove all trace of the Romans. Others, like the Burgundians, tried to preserve Roman buildings. But they didn't have the skills to keep the buildings in good repair.

Each barbarian tribe ruled the area it conquered in its own way. Romans were badly persecuted in some areas. In others the invaders were tolerant. They couldn't keep strict control over large areas, so local Roman governments were able to preserve the Roman way of life for years. But in the West the idea of the empire, which had been so important to the Romans, gradually faded away.

The rise of the Christian Church

In the 4th century AD the Christian Church became richer and more powerful. Educated men chose careers as religious officials rather than entering the army or politics. Bishops, not generals, organized resistance to the barbarians. They also converted many barbarians to Christianity. The developing Church produced many writers and philosophers. Even after the barbarian invasion the Church remained very influential.

This mosaic shows Ambrosius, a Roman bishop respected for his teaching and writings.

As Christianity grew, Christians founded communities called monasteries all over the empire. In monasteries men called monks lived away from the rest of society and observed strict rules of conduct. Some monasteries became famous places of learning, and monks saved and copied ancient books. In this way they preserved many works of Latin and Greek literature and history which otherwise might have been destroyed.

Key dates

AD337-361 Rules of Constantine II, Constans, and Constantius II.

AD361-395 Many emperors of East and West, including Julian ('the Apostate') and Jovian.

AD379-392 Theodosius rules as emperor of East.

AD392-395 Empire reunited under Theodosius.

AD395-423 Rule of Honorius.

AD402 Italy invaded by Alaric the Goth. Honorius moves the imperial court to Ravenna.

AD409 Vandals invade Spain.

AD410 Sack of Rome by Alaric.

AD455 Vandals invade Italy from Africa and destroy Rome.

AD476 Romulus Augustulus, last emperor of the West, is deposed by Odoacer.

The Byzantine empire

While the western half of the empire declined, the eastern half flourished. It preserved many of the traditions of the western Romans, including their administrative skills, military system, and the Christian religion. The eastern empire after the fall of the West became known as the Byzantine empire, after the Greek name for the area.

Constantinople's position (see map) made it an ideal link between Europe and Asia, and it became a powerful city at the heart of a huge empire. The eastern Church became almost

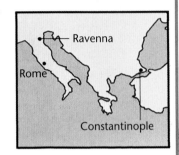

as influential as the Roman Church, and eastern rulers dreamed of reconquering the old Roman empire. Mosaics became very lavish, inlaid with polished glass and precious stones and metals.

This mosaic shows Theodora, the wife of Justinian (see below). Ravenna became the base of the eastern Church in Italy.

Justinian AD527-565

Justinian was one of the greatest emperors of the eastern empire. His armies reconquered most of Rome's former territory in the West. But the cost of this was enormous, and many areas they recovered were delapidated after years of barbarian rule. The inhabitants did not care who ruled them. Except for the southern part of Italy, all the areas that Justinian regained were lost once more within a century.

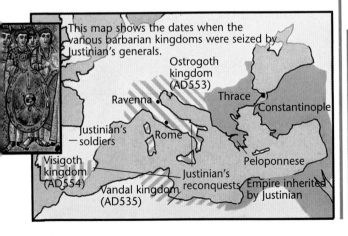

This map shows the dates when the various barbarian kingdoms were seized by Justinian's generals.

Ostrogoth kingdom (AD553)
Ravenna
Thrace
Constantinople
Justinian's soldiers
Rome
Visigoth kingdom (AD554)
Peloponnese
Justinian's reconquests
Vandal kingdom (AD535)
Empire inherited by Justinian

Justinian's achievements

Justinian reorganized the Roman legal system (see pages 74-75), which became the basis of the law in western Europe. He also set about enlarging and enhancing Constantinople. This included building the Church of Santa Sophia (AD534-537). For centuries it was the largest church in the Christian world.

This reconstruction shows Santa Sophia as it might have looked in Byzantine times.

The later Byzantine empire

The eastern empire remained powerful for several centuries, but gradually links with Rome were broken. Latin was replaced by Greek as the official language, and the eastern and Roman Catholic Churches grew apart. The eastern Church was the forerunner of the modern Greek and Russian Orthodox churches.

The empire was soon challenged by Islam, the religion founded in Mecca, Arabia, by the prophet Mohammed (c.AD570-632). Within a century of Mohammed's death much of the old empire had been conquered by the religion's followers, known as Muslims.

The Byzantine empire shrank, until only Thrace and the Peloponnese were left (see map on the left). Constantinople itself was attacked by different invaders and grew weaker and weaker. In AD1453 it fell to the Muslim armies of the Turkish Sultan Mehmet II. This is seen by many historians as the point at which all remaining political links with imperial Rome were finally broken.

Key dates

AD491-518 Rule of Anastasius I, traditionally thought of as the first Byzantine emperor.

AD527-565 Rule of Justinian.

AD528-534 Reorganization of the Roman law (known as the Justinian code).

AD535 Justinian retakes the Vandal kingdom in North Africa.

AD553 Justinian retakes the Ostrogoth kingdom in Italy.

AD555 Justinian retakes the Visigoth kingdom in Spain.

AD1453 Constantinople conquered by Sultan Mehmet II.

Glossary

Many Latin words in this book are explained in this glossary, which also contains some English words that may be unfamiliar. Other, related words appear in **bold** within the text of the entry. When a word is followed by an asterisk, such as senators*, that word has its own entry in this list. When the asterisk sign follows a name, it is listed in the 'Who was who' section, that begins on page 84.

Aedile A government official. Four senators* were elected every year to become *aediles*. They were responsible for markets, streets and public buildings, and also organized public games.

Amphora A large pot with two handles. *Amphorae* were used to transport and store oil and wine.

Amphitheatre A circular or oval building in which gladiator fights and shows of wild beasts took place. The first amphitheatres were wooden; stone ones were later built all over the empire.

Aqueduct A channel or pipe for carrying water. Rome and other cities of the empire had excellent supplies of water which was piped into towns from rivers and springs in the countryside. The pipes were either built underground or set into large bridges – also known as aqueducts – like the Pont du Gard in France.

Assembly A meeting of Roman citizens* in Rome. **Assemblies** were held for various purposes, including the election of government officials, the passing or confirmation of laws, and the declaration of war or peace. The plebeians* also held their own **Popular Assembly**, which excluded patricians*, to elect their own representatives known as tribunes*.

Atrium The central area of a Roman house (*domus**) on to which most of the other rooms opened.

Augustus Imperial title. It was first taken by Octavian* when he became emperor* in 27BC. Later, under the system of succession devised by Nerva*, it was given to each new emperor when he took power. As the Augustus, the emperor chose a successor known as the Caesar*. The two men ruled together until the Augustus died. Then the Caesar took over, became the Augustus, and chose his own Caesar.

Barbarians The name generally given to people who lived outside Roman territory. The Romans saw them as brutal and uncivilized because they did not conform to the Roman way of life. Invasions by various barbarian tribes was one cause of the collapse of the empire.

Basilica A large public building, often near the forum* of a Roman town. It was used as law courts or offices, and sometimes also contained stores and markets.

Bulla A good-luck charm. Each Roman child was given a *bulla* to keep evil spirits away.

Burgundians People, originally from northern Europe, who around AD406 invaded the Roman empire and set up their own kingdom in the province* of Germania.

Caesar Imperial title. Under the scheme of succession devised by Nerva*, each emperor decided who would take his place. The successor, until he himself became emperor, was given the title Caesar.

Cameo A minature carving in semi-precious stone.

Campus Martius The Field of Mars, god of war. An open space near Rome where, in early republican* times, Roman armies assembled to go to war.

Carthage A city on the coast of North Africa founded by the Phoenicians* about 814BC. The growth of **Carthaginian** power in Sicily caused the Punic* wars.

Cavalry The part of an army that fights on horseback.

Censor A government official. Two *censores* were chosen every five years. They served for 18 months; during this period they revised the membership of the Senate* and negotiated contracts for public works.

Census A survey of the population. The Roman government gathered statistics and details about the inhabitants of the empire, mostly for taxation purposes.

Century A unit of the Roman army. At first each century contained 100 men; later this was reduced to 80. Each century was led by an officer known as a **centurion**.

Christianity A religion founded in Palestine by the followers of Jesus of Nazareth (c.5BC-AD29). It spread rapidly through the empire, though **Christians** were often badly persecuted until Christianity became the official state religion around the end of the 4th century AD.

Citizen A Roman man who had the rights to vote and serve in the army. At first, to qualify for **citizenship** people had to be born in Rome to Roman parents. As the empire grew, however, the conditions were changed to include other people. Finally, in AD212, citizenship was granted to all men in the empire except slaves*.

Cohort A unit of the Roman army. After the reforms of Marius*, a cohort became the main tactical unit. In each legion there were 10 cohorts; one contained 10 centuries, the other contained 6 centuries. It was led by an officer known as a *tribunus militum*.

Consul The most senior government official. Two consuls were elected each year; they managed the affairs of the Senate* and commanded the armies.

Contubernium A unit of the Roman army. Each *contubernium* contained eight soldiers who ate together and shared a tent.

Denarius A Roman coin. In early imperial times *denarii* were made from about 4 grams of silver.

Dictator A government official. In times of crisis, such as during a war, the Senate* could appoint a dictator to rule for a maximum of six months. He was given complete control of all other officials and of the army, and took all important military and political decisions.

Domus A private house, normally occupied by one family.

Emperor The supreme ruler of all Roman territories. The first emperor was Augustus*, who took power in 27BC when the Roman republic* collapsed. The period after this date is known as the **Empire** (the capital letter is used in this book to denote 'the **Imperial** period' rather than simply 'Roman territory').

Equites A class of Roman citizen*. The *equites* were descendents of the first Roman cavalry* officers. In later republican* times the term denoted a powerful middle class of businessmen, traders and bankers.

Etruscans People, perhaps originally from Asia Minor, who arrived in Italy around 800BC. The area they inhabited, in northwest and central Italy, is called Etruria. For parts of its very early history, Rome was ruled by Etruscan kings.

Forum An open space in the middle of a Roman town. It was used for markets and trade, and was also the focus of social and political life.

Freed man A slave* who had been released from slavery by his master.

Gauls People who lived mainly to the north and west of Italy. There were many tribes of Gauls, who from around 500BC occupied much of what is now France, and areas as far north as the River Rhine and as far south as the Italian Alps. During the early republic* the Gauls attacked Rome frequently; by Caesar's time, however, most of them had been conquered. Their lands were seized by the Romans to form the various Gallic provinces*.

Goths People who lived originally in Scandinavia. Around the beginning of the 1st century AD they began moving south, and by AD200 they had settled north of the Black Sea. From here they attacked Roman territory in Asia Minor, but were defeated. Shortly after this attack they divided into two factions, known as the Visigoths* and the Ostrogoths*.

Hades Originally, in Greek, the god of the dead. Later, for the Romans, it became the place where a person's spirit went after death. To reach Hades the spirit was rowed across a mythical river called the Styx by a boatman called Charon.

Huns A tribe from eastern Asia who began moving west in the 4th century AD. They invaded the lands of the Ostrogoths*, Visigoths* and Vandals*, who had to move west into the Roman empire to escape them.

Hypocaust A form of central heating used by the Romans. Buildings were constructed with spaces between the inner and outer walls, and below the floors. Fires were lit in special furnaces below the floors and the heat flowed into these cavities.

Insula A block of flats or apartments. Most occupants rented their living quarters from a landlord. Each individual apartment was called a *cenaculum*.

Lararium A shrine, kept either in the *atrium** or garden of a *domus**, containing statues of the Roman household gods. The family said prayers at the *lararium* every day.

Latins People, originally from central Europe, who entered Italy around 2000BC. They settled on the plain of **Latium** (an area of flat land on the northwest plain of the Italian peninsula which surrounds Rome).

Legatus A government official. In republican* times *legati* worked in the provinces*, serving on the staff of the proconsul*. In imperial times *legati* commanded the legions or acted as military and political advisors or administrative assistants.

Legion A unit of the Roman army. The size of the legion varied throughout Rome's history. It is thought that in the earliest times it was made up of about 3,000 soldiers; by the 4th century BC this number had risen to about 4,200. After the reforms of Marius* there were about 5,000 soldiers in a legion.

The number of legions also varied. In later republican* times there were 60, but Augustus* cut this number to 28. After his rule there were always around 30 legions.

Ludi The general name given to Roman sporting events, public games and theatrical performances. Most *ludi* were usually held to mark religious festivals, funerals or battle victories.

Mosaic A picture or abstract pattern made up of small pieces of stone, glass or glazed earthenware.

Nomads People who do not live permanently in any one area but move from place to place.

Ostrogoths A subdivision of the Goths* who built up a huge empire north of the Black Sea in the 3rd and 4th centuries AD. Around AD370 they were overrun by the Huns*, and so had to move west. From around AD455 they lived in the Balkans. They overran Italy in AD489, led by Theoderic, who deposed the barbarian ruler Odoacer and then declared himself king of Italy.

Paedagogus A slave*, often Greek, employed by Roman parents to look after their children at school.

Papyrus A reed used to make a form of writing material (itself often also called papyrus). It was cut into strips which were pressed, dried and polished to create a smooth writing surface.

Patricians A class of Roman citizen*, Patricians were descended from the oldest families of Roman noblemen. In early republican* times, only patrician men were allowed to become senators*. They also held all the most important political, religious and legal appointments.

Peristylium A row of columns round a building or open space. The word is also used to mean an outdoor walkway or garden surrounded by a row of columns.

Phoenicians People who lived in the eastern Mediterranean (now Lebanon) from around 1200BC. They were avid traders and seafarers, and rapidly occupied many Mediterranean islands and parts of North Africa. Their most important colony was Carthage. The growth of Carthaginian power in Sicily caused the Punic* wars.

Plebeians A class of Roman people. The plebeians were the poorest citizens* who were probably descended from Rome's first farmers and traders.

Praetor A government official. At first the word was used for the two most important officials who replaced the kings at the beginning of the republic*. Later these men became known as consuls*; the word *praetor* instead came to mean the senior judges, administrative officers elected each year by the Assembly*, and governors in some of the provinces*.

Praetorian Guard An army of around 9,000 soldiers formed by Augustus*. It protected Italy and the emperor, as there were no legions* to do this. Because it was the only army stationed in Rome, it became very powerful.

Proconsul A government official. A proconsul was a consul* who, after his term of office, was sent by the Senate* to another job, usually as governor in one of the provinces*.

Province From later republican* times (after the expansion of Roman territory), any area outside Rome (later outside Italy) that was controlled by the Romans. The inhabitants of these areas are known as **provincials**.

Punic wars Three wars, fought at intervals from 264BC to 146BC, between the Romans and the Carthaginians. The word Punic is derived from the Latin word *Punicus*, meaning Phoenician*.

Quaestor A government official. Twenty **quaestores** were chosen each year to be financial administrators.

Republic A state or country without a king, queen or emperor which is governed by elected representatives of the people. Rome became a republic at the beginning of the 6th century BC when the last Etruscan* king was expelled. Though after this it was occasionally ruled by dictators*, it remained a republic until 27BC when Octavian* became emperor*.

Senate The group of officials that governed Rome. In early republican* times the Senate consisted of around 100 patricians*; by 82BC there were 600 **senators**, selected from all classes of citizen*. The Senate took most political, military and legal decisions that related to Rome and Roman territory, but gradually the **senatorial** system broke down. After a period of dictatorships* and civil wars, Octavian* took power. During imperial times, the Senate's powers were gradually reduced as emperors took more and more power for themselves.

Slave A person owned by another and used as a worker. In Rome, most slaves were non-Romans, such as prisoners of war and their descendants. They were owned by citizens* or by the state, and were bought and sold like any other property. They had no rights or privileges.

Terracotta A mixture of clay and sand, baked to make tiles and small statues.

Toga The official garment of a Roman citizen*. It was a roughly semi-circular piece of wool cloth which the wearer draped around his body in an elaborate series of folds. Plain white was most popular; senators wore a *toga* with a purple border. Young boys also wore a *toga* with a purple hem, known as the *toga praetexta*.

Tribune An official elected by the plebeians* to represent them in the Senate* and protect their interests. In the first Popular Assembly* of 494BC two tribunes were elected; later this number was increased to ten. Tribunes could prevent any actions of the Senate or laws passed by magistrates if they believed that these threatened the rights of the plebeians.

Vandals People who lived originally in Scandinavia. At the end of the 1st century BC they began moving south; by around AD200 they occupied an area southwest of the River Danube. In AD406, moving west to avoid the Huns*, they crossed the River Rhine into Gaul and devastated large areas of the country. In AD409 they entered Spain, where some of them settled; others moved on to North Africa. From here they sailed to Italy and in AD455 attacked and destroyed Rome.

Viaduct A bridge built to carry a road across a river or a valley.

Villa A large house in the country. Most villas were owned by rich city-dwellers who only visited the country from time to time. When the owner was absent the estate was run by a manager. Many villas were attached to farms or other industries.

Visigoths A subdivision of the Goths* who settled in Dacia in the 3rd century AD. In AD376, escaping from the Huns*, they moved south across the River Danube and into Moesia. Led by Alaric, they advanced through Greece, continuing to Italy and in AD419 attacked Rome. After this they moved to Gaul, and finally settled in Spain, where their kingdom survived until the 8th century AD.

Who was who in ancient Rome

Here you can find out more about important Romans. If a name is in **bold** in the text of an entry, that person has his or her own entry in this list. Words with an asterisk* are in the glossary.

Agrippina (AD15-59) Mother of **Nero**. She became involved in various political intrigues and was eventually banished from Rome in AD39. Her uncle Claudius, however, allowed her to return to Rome and married her in AD49. She encouraged him to adopt Nero, her son by a previous marriage. It is said that she later poisoned Claudius so that Nero could become emperor. Later, when she opposed Nero's intention to marry Poppaea Sabina, Nero had her murdered.

Augustus The title taken in 27BC by Octavian when he became the first Roman emperor*.

Octavian (63BC-AD14) was the great-nephew and adopted son of Julius **Caesar**. After Caesar's death he formed an alliance with **Mark Antony** and Lepidus; the three men seized power and in 42BC defeated **Brutus** and his troops. When Lepidus retired, Octavian and Antony split Roman territory between them, but later disagreed. Octavian defeated Antony in the Battle of Actium in 31BC.

After so many years of civil war the Senate knew that Rome needed a strong ruler to take charge, so they gave Octavian command of the armies, sole control of foreign policy, and the power to reform the Roman administration. He was given the title Augustus ('revered one') in recognition of his status as the head of the Roman government.

By working closely with the Senate and involving it in his decisions Augustus brought peace and prosperity to the Roman world after decades of unrest and civil war. In addition he reformed the army and made the provinces more secure. Building schemes were begun in Rome, and welfare was improved for the poor. According to **Suetonius**, Augustus was fair and honest; his rule was so successful that the idea of restoring a republican* government gradually died out.

Brutus (85-42BC) Politician, and leader of the plot to assassinate **Caesar**. A famous soldier, and a firm believer in the ideals of the Roman republic*, he thought that Caesar was far too powerful. Hoping to restore republican traditions, he and several others murdered Caesar in 44BC. After this he fled to Macedonia and later committed suicide.

Caesar, Julius Gaius (c.100-44BC) Politician, general and writer. He was born in Rome, and was educated there and later in Rhodes in Greece. He joined the army and already had a reputation as a fine soldier when his political career began in 68BC. From 58BC to 49BC he led Roman troops as far as the Atlantic coast and the English Channel. He recorded this period of his life, and details of his military campaigns, in seven books named *De Bello Gallico* (About the Gallic Wars).

Disputes with Pompey and the Senate caused Caesar to return to Italy in 49BC, supported by his army. After defeating various enemies he became the most powerful man in Rome. He described these victories in three books named *De Bello Civili* (About the Civil Wars). He was declared dictator* for life, but despite his popularity with the Roman people, many senators believed he was much too powerful. A group of these, led by **Brutus**, murdered him on 15 March 44BC.

Caligula See **Gaius**.

Cato (234-149BC) Politician and writer. He fought in the second Punic* war, and afterwards held various political positions in Sicily, Africa and Sardinia. In 184BC he was a censor*. Cato believed in the republican* values established when Rome was a small, semi-rural settlement: restraint, dignity, and simple living. These are described in his book *De Agri Cultura*, which is the oldest work of Latin prose which has survived. He also wrote *Origines*, a history of the Roman people from the earliest times. His great grandson, also a politician, was one of Caesar's bitterest enemies.

Catullus (c.84-c.54BC) Poet. He settled in Rome as a young man. Details of his life, including travels to Asia and his final illness, are recorded in his poems. These include laments, witty parodies and elegant descriptions of incidents from Roman life. Catullus was one of the first Roman poets to adopt the forms and styles of Greek poetry.

Cicero (106-43BC) Politician, lawyer and writer. He was educated in Rome and then Athens, and in 81BC his first speeches in the law courts earned him recognition as the greatest public speaker of his day. He became a famous lawyer, and was a consul* in 63BC. He made political enemies, however, by speaking out against people in the Senate and courts. After **Caesar** was murdered Cicero made many speeches in the Senate opposing **Mark Antony**. As a result, when Antony and **Octavian** took power, Cicero was murdered by their troops.

Many of Cicero's speeches were written down; they tell us a lot about life in Rome in late republican* times. His letters and philosophical writings also survive, and show that Cicero was responsible for introducing many Greek ideas to the Romans. His style of writing and public speaking were imitated by scholars for centuries after his death.

Claudius (10BC-AD54) Emperor AD41-54. He was declared emperor by the army after the death of **Gaius**. Childhood illnesses had left him weak and crippled, and most of his relatives thought him stupid. But he was in fact very intelligent; contemporary accounts tell us he was a good public speaker, an excellent historian (he wrote several books of history, though none survives) and a wise and sympathetic ruler.

Constantine (c.AD274-337) Emperor AD312-337. He was leading the army in England when his father, the emperor Constantius, died. Constantine returned to Rome and defeated his rival for the throne, Maxentius, at the Milvian Bridge. Once in power he moved the imperial court from Rome to a new city on the Black Sea which he called Constantinople (now Istanbul). Constantine was the first Christian emperor; in AD313 he issued the Edict of Milan, granting freedom of worship to Christians.

Crassus (c.112-53BC) Soldier and politician. He defeated the uprising led by the slave Spartacus in 71BC, and was consul with **Pompey** the following year. In 60BC he joined an alliance with Pompey and **Caesar**; his extreme wealth enabled him to support Caesar's political amibitions.

Diocletian (AD245-313) Emperor AD284-305. He was declared emperor in AD284 by his troops. He made many radical reforms to coinage, taxation, the army and, most importantly, the way in which the empire was organized. After splitting Roman territory into two he ruled the East and appointed another emperor, Maximian, to rule the West. The administrative systems he devised, implemented by an expanded civil service, lasted for centuries.

Domitian (AD51-96) Emperor AD81-96. He took power after the death of his brother **Titus**, and quickly began to strengthen the frontiers of the empire to protect them from the barbarians. A patron of the arts, he also restored and improved many of Rome's buildings. But he was an arrogant ruler who did not respect the Senate. The end of his rule was marked by constant political quarrels. He solved these by ordering the murder of anyone who disagreed with him. He was eventually assassinated.

Gaius (AD12-41) Emperor AD37-41. He grew up in various military camps by the Rhine river, where his father was an officer. He was nicknamed Caligula because he wore small soldier's boots (*caligulae*) as a child. **Suetonius** and others describe him as arrogant, cruel and extravagant. After ruling for four years in a wilful, inconsistent manner he was murdered by the Praetorian Guard*.

Hadrian (AD76-138) Emperor AD117-138. He succeeded his relative and adoptive father **Trajan**. A great soldier, he spent much of his rule with the armies in the provinces, and set up permanent barriers against the barbarians, including Hadrian's Wall in Britain. He was also a scholar and patron of the arts. He built a library in Athens and a villa for himself at Tibur near Rome. Around AD135 he set up an organization called the Athenaeum to sponsor writers and philosophers.

Horace (65-8BC) Poet. He was educated in Rome and Athens, then worked in Rome as a government clerk and began writing poetry. He became very friendly with **Virgil**, and with Maecaenas, a patron of poets, who gave him a farm where he settled to write his poetry. **Augustus** asked Horace to be his secretary, but he refused. From their letters, however, it appears that the two men were good friends. Horace's most famous works are the *Odes*, short poems on various subjects including the joys of the countryside, food and wine. His poetry became famous almost immediately and has remained widely read and studied.

Julian (AD332-363) Emperor AD360-363. On becoming emperor he began to restore worship of the ancient Roman deities, going against the official religion of the state which was by that time Christianity. He is known as 'the Apostate' – someone who abandons one religion for another. He greatly reduced the palace staff and improved the civil service, but was unpopular because of his religious views. He was killed fighting in Persia. Some of his letters and other writings survive, which give us details of political and religious life at that time.

Justinian (c.AD482-565) Emperor of the East, AD527-565. His most important political achievement was to recapture many of the territories in the West that had been overrun by barbarians. He also commissioned a huge reorganization of the Roman legal system, which formed the basis of his reforms of the political administration.

Juvenal (c.AD60-130) Poet. Almost nothing is known about his life. The first of his poems still in existence were probably published around AD110. His works are called *Satires*; they criticize what Juvenal saw as the evils and defects of life in Rome – poverty, immorality and injustice. The attacks, though bitter, are delivered with biting wit. It is thought that his poems led to him being banished from Rome for a time.

Livia (58BC-AD29) Wife of **Augustus**, and, by an earlier marriage, mother of **Tiberius**. She was an aristocrat from one of the oldest Roman families, and had considerable influence on Augustus's rule. Roman historians tell us she was shrewd and wise; it is possible that she persuaded Augustus against his will to appoint Tiberius as his successor.

Livy (59BC-AD17) Historian. He spent much of his life in Rome writing *Ab Urbe Condita*, a huge history of the city and its people. It was published in instalments and made him very wealthy and famous. It charts the development of Rome from the earliest times, and provides us with much detail of both historical incidents and everyday life in the city.

Marcus Aurelius (AD121-180) Emperor AD161-180. Much of his rule was spent at the empire's frontiers, trying to keep barbarian tribes out. Aurelius's journals, known as *Meditations* and written mostly in army camps, show him to have been a peace-loving, philosophical man.

Marius (157-86BC) Soldier and politician. He fought successful campaigns in Spain, Africa and Gaul. During this period he was appointed consul* six times (107BC, 104-100BC) and used his power to reorganize the army and make it more efficient. After this he was hardly involved in political life until 88BC, when tensions arose between him and **Sulla**. The struggle for power between the two men was one of the causes of the civil war that brought about the collapse of the Roman republic*. Marius seized control in 87BC and the following year was appointed consul for the seventh time just before his death.

Mark Antony (82-30BC) Soldier and politician. He was a consul* with **Caesar** in 44BC. After Caesar's death he formed an alliance with **Octavian**; they split Roman territory and Antony ruled Egypt with his lover Cleopatra, the Egyptian queen. Later the two men disagreed and war broke out between them. Antony and Cleopatra committed suicide after their defeat by Octavian at the Battle of Actium.

Martial (c.AD40-104) Poet. He was born in Spain, and lived in Rome for many years. His poems, known as *Epigrams*, provide details of everyday life and describe some of Rome's more entertaining characters. While much of his work is bitterly satirical, attacking various individuals for their faults, his writings also include poems to his friends and touching laments.

Nero (AD37-68) Emperor AD54-68. At first Nero's rule was effective and stable, but he freed himself from the influence of his advisors (including **Seneca**) and became arrogant and obsessed with power. Anone who opposed him was murdered (including his mother **Agrippina**). According to **Suetonius** he sponsored public shows and games in which he himself appeared, and had to increase taxes to pay for them. It is thought that he caused the fire that destroyed much of Rome in AD64, and then began the organized persecution of Christians, blaming them for the blaze. Eventually he left Rome and was forced to commit suicide.

Nerva (c.AD30-98) Emperor, AD96-98. He was appointed emperor by the Senate after **Domitian** was assassinated. A highly respected lawyer, he restored faith in imperial rule by treating the Senate and others officials with consideration. The army, at first uneasy about his appointment, was won over when he chose a famous soldier, **Trajan**, to succeed him. Nerva is best remembered for devising this system of succession (after him each emperor chose and trained his own replacement), and for increasing aid to the poor.

Octavian See **Augustus**.

Ovid (43BC-AD18) Poet. He was educated in Rome and studied to become a lawyer, but gave this up to write poetry. His work became very popular in Rome, and he was friendly with **Horace** and others. In AD8, however, he was banished to the shore of the Black Sea by Augustus; the reason for this is not entirely clear, but he never returned to Rome. His most famous work is *Metamorphoses*, fifteen books of poems on a variety of subjects, chiefly legends or myths, all involving changes of shape and character. Ovid's poetry is notable for its pictorial detail; his writing later influenced many artists, including Rubens and Picasso.

Petronius Arbiter (lived 1st century AD) Author. Little is known about his life, but several of his works survive. The most famous of these is the *Satyricon*, a rambling narrative about the experience of three characters as they travel through southern Italy. The work is most important as a report on the social customs of the day, and as a description of the lives of people of various classes; it also contains historical poems and snatches of political commentary.

Plautus (c.254-184BC) Playwright. He is said to have written more than 130 plays, though only 21 survive. These are all based on Greek comedies, but introduce features of Roman life, often affectionately parodied, probably to make them more interesting to Roman audiences. The works of Plautus have inspired many later playwrights, particularly Shakespeare and Molière.

Pliny (c.AD61-c.113) Writer and lawyer. During **Trajan**'s rule he served as a consul*. He published nine volumes of his correspondence with the emperor, his friend **Tacitus** and others. Written in a clear, elegant style, they are an excellent source of information about the Roman world at that time.

Plutarch (AD46-126) Writer. He was born in Greece, but later lived in Rome. Many of his writings survive. They cover several different subjects, including science, literature and philosophy. His more famous work, known in English as *Plutarch's Lives*, is a series of biographies of Greek and Roman soldiers and statesmen. They are grouped in pairs, one Greek, one Roman, and their lives and careers are carefully compared.

Pompey (106-48BC) Soldier and politician. He fought with **Sulla** against **Marius**, and later suppressed the rebellion of discontented slaves led by Spartacus. Asia Minor became part of Roman territory as a result of his campaigns there. He joined an alliance with **Caesar** and **Crassus** in 60BC, and remained in Rome while Caesar was fighting in Gaul. Because of growing political tensions, however, the alliance broke down, and in 49BC Caesar returned to Rome and seized power. Pompey was later defeated and died in Egypt.

Seneca (c.5BC-AD65) Writer, philosopher and lawyer. He was born in Spain, but spent most of his life in Rome. In AD41 he was banished from Rome by **Claudius**, but was recalled by Agrippina eight years later to be **Nero**'s tutor. For a time Nero governed well, probably because of Seneca's influence, but the administration deteriorated and in AD62, Seneca asked to retire. Three years later he was accused of conspiracy against Nero and was forced to commit suicide. Seneca's most famous works are the *Apocolocyntosis*, a satire describing the deification of the emperor Claudius, and *Moral Letters*, about his philosophical beliefs.

Sibyl A name used by the Greek and Roman peoples for several prophetesses active all over the Ancient World. One of them offered nine books of her prophecies to Rome's early king Tarquinius Priscus. When he refused to buy them, she burned three of the books and offered him the remaining six. Priscus refused again; the Sibyl burned another three books and offered the king the last three at the original price for nine. Priscus bought the books, which were kept in Rome by special priests; they were thought to be so sacred that they could only be consulted in extreme emergencies.

Suetonius (c.AD69-140) Historian. After a period as a lawyer he became a government assistant to **Trajan**, Hadrian and others. His most famous work is *Lives of the Twelve Caesars*, which has survived in complete form. It discusses the careers of each Roman ruler from **Caesar** to **Domitian**. As well as studying the political careers of the emperors, it also passes on a wealth of detail about their different personalities, appearances, families and habits. In addition Suetonius also recorded the gossip and scandal surrounding the lives of his subjects.

Sulla (138-78BC) General and politician. His first military successes were as a lieutenant to **Marius**, who later became his fiercest rival. Between 88 and 86BC the two men were involved in constant struggles for power; after Marius's death in 86BC Sulla and his troops seized control of Rome and he declared himself dictator*. A man of highly conservative views, he tried to return power to the Senate and the patricians*.

Tacitus (c.AD55-116) Historian. He served as a military officer and held several different government posts, including consul*. According to contemporary sources Tacitus was an excellent public speaker. His most famous works are the *Annals* (about the period from **Tiberius**'s rule to the death of **Nero**) and the *Histories* (about the lives of the Roman emperors from Galba to **Domitian**).

Terence (c.195-159BC) Playwright. Terence was originally a slave*, but was freed by his master. His six plays – including *Phormio* and *Adelphoe* – were adapted from Greek comedy. According to some contemporary sources, many Roman audiences of the day found Terence's plays dull, possibly because they found them to be less exuberant than those of the Roman playwright **Plautus**. But Terence's work was performed in imperial times, and was also known in the Middle Ages. Many famous later writers, including Sheridan and Molière, were inspired by his plays.

Tiberius (42BC-AD37) Emperor AD14-37. He had already retired to Rhodes when he was recalled to Rome in AD2. Twelve years later he became emperor. He appears to have been an excellent administrator, but many of his reforms were very unpopular with the people of Rome. Terrified of being assassinated, he withdrew to the island of Capri and ruled through his deputy, Sejanus. Eventually Sejanus tried to seize power for himself, and Tiberius had him executed. After this he became suspicious and tyrannical. Anyone who he thought opposed him was forced to commit suicide.

Titus (AD39-81) Emperor AD79-81. He was the elder son of **Vespasian**, and had a distinguished military career. His capture of Jerusalem in AD70 is depicted on a triumphal arch in Rome known as the Arch of Titus. According to **Suetonius** he was extremely popular, generous and merciful. He gave financial aid to people who had suffered in the volcanic eruptions at Herculaneum and Pompeii (AD79) and in a huge fire in Rome (AD80). The Colosseum in Rome and other public buildings were completed during his term of office.

Trajan (c.AD53-117) Emperor AD98-117. He was born in Spain and was an outstanding soldier and general; his military successes are commemorated on a huge sculpted pillar in Rome known as Trajan's Column. During his rule the empire grew to its largest with the conquest of Dacia and Parthia. Among his public works at Rome were baths, markets, a basilica and a new forum.

Vespasian (AD9-79) Emperor AD70-79. He came to power after the murder of **Nero** and the short rules of Galba, Otho and Vitellius. Rome was in civil and financial turmoil, but he quickly restored order. His improvements of the administration and the army achieved political stability, and he began an extensive campaign of public building. This included the Colosseum, temples and restorations to the forum and elsewhere.

Virgil (70-19BC) Poet. He was educated at Cremona, Milan and Rome. His first published work, the *Eclogues*, is a series of poems about life in the country. In 42BC his land was confiscated to provide farms for retired soldiers, and he lived for a time near Rome, and later near Naples and elsewhere. He completed his next great poems, the *Georgics*, in 30BC. During the last 10 years of his life he worked on the *Aeneid*, a poem in twelve books about the hero Aeneas and the origin of the Roman empire.

Vitruvius (c.70BC-early 1st century AD) Architect and engineer. Vitruvius is most famous as the author of *De Architectura*, a series of ten books about architecture and building. The books include information about civil engineering, construction, town planning and materials, and there are also sections about the different techniques and styles of decoration. *De Architectura* brought together lots of information about ancient Greek architecture and design, and is the only work of its kind to have survived ancient times.

Date chart

This chart lists the most important dates in Roman history. It also includes some events that took place elsewhere in the world during the same period; these are shown in *italics*.

Dates BC

from c.2000BC Immigrants enter Italy from the North.

c.900BC First settlements on Palatine and Esquiline hills.

c.900BC State of Sparta founded in Greece.

c.800BC Etruscans arrive in Italy by sea.

776BC First Olympic Games held in Greece.

753BC Date traditionally given for the founding of Rome.

c.750BC Greek migrants settle in southern Italy and Sicily.

c.650BC First coinage appears in Lydia (Asia Minor).

510 or 509BC Last king expelled; Roman republic begins.

c.505BC Democracy established in Athens by Cleisthenes.

496BC Romans defeated by an alliance of Latin cities at the Battle of Lake Regillus.

494BC Plebeians go on strike for the first time.

493BC First two tribunes appointed.

490BC Battle of Marathon; Persians defeated by Greeks.

450BC Publication of Roman laws called the Twelve Tables.

449BC Number of tribunes increased to ten.

431-404BC Peloponnesian War between Athens and Sparta.

by 400BC Rome is dominant partner in Latin alliance.

367BC New law states that one consul must be a plebeian.

366BC First plebeian consul is elected.

338BC Romans defeat the other members of the Latin alliance; the alliance is terminated.

334BC Alexander the Great invades Asia Minor. He conquers Egypt in 332, Persia in 330 and India in 329.

326BC War between the Romans and the Samnites.

323BC Death of Alexander the Great in Babylon.

312BC The Appian Way is begun.

287BC Lex Hortensia passed, stating that all resolutions of the Popular Assembly should become law.

286BC Final defeat of the Samnites.

280-272BC Pyrrhic wars.

by 264BC Rome dominates the whole of Italy.

264-241BC First Punic war.

241BC Sicily becomes the first Roman province.

238BC Romans seize Sardinia.

220BC Via Flamina built.

218-202BC Second Punic war.

214BC Great Wall built in China.

204BC Rome invades Africa.

202BC Rome seizes Carthaginian territory in Spain.

179BC First stone bridge built over the Tiber river.

149-146BC Third Punic war ends with fall of Carthage.

133BC Rome acquires the province of Asia. Tiberius Gracchus becomes tribune.

123BC Gaius Gracchus becomes tribune.

121BC Province of Gallia Narbonensis acquired.

107BC Marius becomes consul and reforms the army.

88BC Sulla marches on Rome and drives Marius into exile.

87BC Marius recaptures Rome, but dies the following year.

82-80BC Sulla is dictator.

73-71BC Rebellion of slaves, led by Spartacus.

70BC Crassus and Pompey are consuls.

63BC Pompey acquires provinces of Bythnia, Pontus, Cyrene, Syria and Crete.

59BC Caesar is consul.

58-49BC Caesar's campaigns in Gaul.

55-54BC Caesar's invasions of Britain.

53BC Death of Crassus.

49BC Caesar seizes power in Rome. Civil war begins between him and the Senate's forces (led by Pompey).

48BC Pompey is killed in battle.

45BC Caesar defeats the Senate's forces and becomes sole leader of the Roman world.

44BC Caesar is assassinated by Brutus and Cassius.

42BC Deaths of Brutus and Cassius.

c.33BC Growing tension between Octavian and Mark Antony leads to civil war.

31BC Octavian defeats Antony and Cleopatra at the Battle of Actium.

27BC Octavian becomes first Roman emperor, and is given the title Augustus.

c.5BC Birth of Jesus Christ in Bethlehem, Judaea.

Dates AD

AD14 Death of Augustus. Tiberius becomes Emperor.

AD14-37 Rule of Tiberius.

AD17 Death of the historian Livy.

AD37-41 Rule of Caligula.

AD41-54 Rule of Claudius.

AD43 Conquest of Britain.

AD54-68 Rule of Nero.

AD64 Fire of Rome; Nero begins persecution of Christians.

AD68-69 After Nero's death, power struggles lead to civil wars.

AD69 Reigns of Galba, Otho and Vitellius.

AD69-79 Rule of Vespasian.

AD79 The Colosseum in Rome is opened.

AD79-81 Rule of Titus.

AD79 The volcano Vesuvius erupts, destroying the towns of Herculaneum and Pompeii on the west coast of Italy.

AD81-96 Rule of Domitian.

AD96-98 Rule of Nerva.

AD98-117 Rule of Trajan.

AD112 Trajan's forum in Rome is completed.

AD117 The empire reaches its largest extent after the conquests of Dacia and Parthia.

AD117-138 Rule of Hadrian.

AD122 Hadrian's Wall and other frontiers begun.

AD138-161 Rule of Antoninus Pius.

AD161-180 Rule of Marcus Aurelius.

AD180-192 Rule of Commodus.

AD193-211 Rule of Septimius Severus.

AD211-217 Rule of Caracalla.

AD212 Roman citizenship for all free people in the empire.

AD217-218 Rule of Macrinus.

AD218-222 Rule of Elagabalus.

AD222-235 Rule of Severus Alexander.

AD235-284 Short reigns of many emperors.

AD260-275 Gaul declares independence from Rome.

AD270 Romans begin to abandon parts of the empire.

AD271-275 The Aurelian Wall is built around Rome.

AD284 Diocletian splits empire into East and West.

AD284-305 Rule of Diocletian (East).

AD286-305 Rule of Maximinian (West).

AD286 Britain declares itself independent from Rome.

AD301 Edict of prices issued to regulate inflation.

AD305-312 Rule of Constantius I, followed by struggles for power which end when Constantine defeats Maxentius at the Battle of the Milvian Bridge.

AD312-337 Rule of Constantine. Empire reunited from AD324.

AD313 Constantine tolerates Christian worship.

AD330 Constantine moves his court to Byzantium, where he founds the city of Constantinople.

AD337 Constantine baptized into Christian faith.

AD337-361 Rule of Constantine's sons.

AD361-363 Rule of Julian the Apostate; state religion restored.

AD363-364 Rule of Jovian. Christianity restored.

AD364-379 Rules of Valentinian I, Valens, Gratian, Valentinian II.

AD367 Barbarian tribes, moving west to escape the Huns, begin to set up their own kingdoms on Roman territory.

AD379-392 Theodosius rules as emperor of the East.

AD392-395 Empire reunited under Theodosius.

AD394 Christianity becomes official state religion.

AD395-423 Rule of Honorius.

AD402 Goths invade Italy. Honorius moves to Ravenna.

AD406 The River Rhine freezes, allowing the Goths to cross it and enter Roman territory.

AD409 Vandals invade Spain.

AD410 Sack of Rome by Alaric the Goth. Rome abandons territories in Britain and Gaul.

AD455 Vandals invade Italy from Africa and destroy Rome.

AD475 Visigoths declare an independent kingdom in Spain.

AD476 Romulus Augustulus, last emperor of the West, is deposed by Odoacer, a barbarian captain who declares himself king of Italy.

AD491-518 Rule of Anastasius I, traditionally thought of as the first Byzantine emperor.

AD527-565 Rule of Justinian.

AD535-555 Justinian's troops recapture much of the empire from the barbarians, but these territories are later lost again.

AD1453 Constantinople is conquered by Sultan Mehmet II.

The legacy of Rome

The Roman empire in western Europe came to a close in AD476 when the last emperor in Italy, Romulus Augustulus, was deposed. But the Roman way of life was so widespread and firmly established that it did not simply disappear when the barbarians took over. Some elements of Roman civilization remained as strong as ever and had a huge impact on later cultures. Other aspects of Roman life – chiefly ideas and literature – all but disappeared in the Middle Ages. But they were maintained for centuries in monasteries and other places of learning until they were rediscovered by writers, artists and scholars.

The Romans also transmitted to us skills and ideas learned or borrowed from other ancient cultures. Without the Romans, much information about more remote civilizations would be lost. Greek sculptures and many Greek writings exist almost solely in the form of Roman copies. Below are examples of the ways in which the influence of the Roman world continues to be felt today.

Towns and cities

Much of western Europe had no urban civilization before the Romans, and they profoundly influenced its geography. They nearly always chose excellent positions for their towns, assessing physical and political factors before beginning to build. Many modern cities occupy the sites they do only because the Romans built there first. These include London, Paris, Lyons, Bordeaux, Cologne, Toledo, Milan and, of course, Rome itself.

Some European towns are still laid out as the Romans planned them, with a large open space in the middle corresponding to the *forum* and roads that intersect at right angles. Bridges, markets and other public landmarks often occupy the sites where the Romans first placed them. In addition, other cities built or rebuilt long after Roman times were created by town planners in imitation of the grid pattern of the Greeks and Romans; these include New York and Lisbon.

Travel and communications

The Romans established trade and military routes in Europe and into North Africa and Asia. Many can still be seen in ruins; far more form the basis of modern main roads and rail routes, though the Roman structures no longer exist. In addition, the wheel guage of Roman wagons became fixed at around 143cm (just over 4ft) once ruts were worn in their roads. This is now the width of many trains, as early steam trains were tested on tracks in mines developed by the Romans.

Architecture

Very few barbarian tribes were able to maintain Roman buildings, and some actually destroyed them. Cities fell into disrepair and were plundered for stone and marble. But many Roman buildings lasted because they were so well made. The Romans' innovations and developments in architecture and building technology – the arch, the dome and the use of concrete – enabled them to create huge structures that still survive today. Some are still in use, like the Pantheon in Rome and theatres and amphitheatres all over southern Europe.

In places where building continued after Roman times, such as parts of the Eastern empire and certain cities in Italy, architects at first imitated the great buildings of Rome. Later in the Byzantine world architectural styles gradually changed, but many buildings were still based on the large domes and basilicas of late Roman times. In addition, many Roman basilicas were turned into churches during this period.

During the Renaissance (see opposite) Italian architects like Palladio (1518-80) discovered the books of the Roman architect Vitruvius. These set out the rules and styles of the classical architecture of Greece and Rome. Renaissance architects followed these guidelines; some copied Roman buildings in their entirety, others incorporated the rules into new designs. In addition, at this time many original Roman buildings were restored. The Baths of Diocletian in Rome, for example, were turned into the church of Santa Maria degli Angeli by the Renaissance artist Michelangelo.

Though new styles of architecture later developed, many architects continued to use Greek and Roman principles of proportion and design. In the 19th century many civic monuments were built with columns, domes and arched halls in an attempt to capture the imposing grandeur of ancient Rome. The National Gallery in London and the Louvre in Paris are good examples. Some large state buildings in the USA, including the Capitol in Washington, DC, also follow this style.

Painting and sculpture

In Renaissance times artists became fascinated with the classical statues (mostly Greek but preserved in Roman copies) that were being rediscovered. Michelangelo and others adopted their realistic style and their proportions and moods, often altering them subtly to suit their own purposes. Myths and legends from the classical world were often used as the subject for paintings by such artists as Botticelli. At that stage, however, very few Roman wall-paintings had been found; when, in the 18th century, excavations began at Pompeii, classically inspired painting and sculpture received a fresh impetus. The classical legacy remains a source of inspiration for many modern artists.

Language

When the Romans conquered a new area, its inhabitants had to learn the language of their conquerors, because the new administration was conducted in Latin. This was not the language of literature or public speaking but the everyday speech of peasants and soldiers. It survived after the fall of the empire, spoken all over the Roman world in various provincial forms. These dialects, when they fused with the languages of the barbarian invaders, grew into the modern European languages. Many of them – particularly Portuguese, Italian, French, Spanish and Romanian – are very closely linked to Latin. Others, like English, are more distantly related, but still contain thousands of Latin words.

A more formal, official Latin was preserved by the Christian Church. All church ceremonies were conducted in Latin, and it was the language spoken in monasteries, As these places were the main places of learning during the Middle Ages, Latin became the language of scholars. By the 16th century Latin was used all over Europe by scholars, diplomats and scientists. This tradition has survived into modern times; a qualification in Latin is often recognized as a good training, even for jobs that are totally unrelated to it.

Law

The Roman legal system survived the collapse of the empire for many reasons. It was widely established, well integrated into society on a local level, and meticulously documented. The Romans' idea of justice and rights, as outlined in the Justinian Code (AD528-534), remains relevant today. Some modern legal systems, such as that in France, are based in a large part on the Justinian Code; others, though now very different, still display their origins in the Roman system. In the USA, the state law of Louisiana still follows Roman law closely.

Government

The concept of an empire – a territory unified by one set of laws and governed by a central body – was not a Roman invention. The Macedonian ruler Alexander the Great conquered large parts of the eastern Mediterranean and Asia, hoping to unite them under a single political administration, but died before he could carry this out. The Romans not only acquired a vast empire but also succeeded in governing it smoothly and effectively. The Romans brought many benefits to the areas they conquered: improved buildings, trade, a legal system, and the vast economic resources of the empire.

The imperialist system was later copied by many rulers, with varying degrees of success. In AD800 Charlemagne, King of the Franks, was also crowned 'Emperor of the Romans', in imitation of earlier Roman rulers.

Later Frankish and German leaders continued this tradition, and named their territories the Holy Roman Empire. This institution remained in existence in Germany until 1806.

In the 18th century the revolutionary movements in France and America were inspired by the ideals of the Roman republic to overthrow monarchic rule. The USA is still governed by a body called the Senate. By the 19th century some European countries had empires all over the world, to which they, like the Romans, tried to export their culture and governmental systems. In modern times the European Union can be seen as an extension of the Roman ideal; it aims to bring member states together with a common monetary and taxation system, a central government, and an international court of justice.

Elements of Roman government survive today in the Roman Catholic Church. Its managerial units, known as dioceses, were invented by Diocletian for civic purposes and only later adopted by the church. The idea of a religious empire with a leader – the Pope – and its own laws is derived from the Roman imperial administration.

Literature and ideas

Latin literature, and histories of the Romans written by Romans themselves, were preserved in the Middle Ages by monks, who collected ancient books and copied the original manuscripts. From the 13th century there was a steady drift to the West of monks from the crumbling Byzantine world. The books they brought with them provoked new interest in Greece and Rome; this in turn brought about cultural changes in Europe known collectively as the Renaissance.

The Renaissance influenced all aspects of European life. Greek and Roman writings taught Renaissance thinkers to stress human possibilities rather than dwell, as most Medieval theorists did, on human failings. Learning began to develop independently of the Church; schools and universities were founded by bankers and others in non-religious walks of life. Scientists and medical experiments flourished. The political, religious and technological changes mark the end of the Medieval age.

Renaissance poets like Petrarch and Boccaccio imitated Latin verse forms; the Dutch scholar Erasmus perfected his Latin prose style by detailed study of Cicero. In this way writers incorporated Latin styles and ideas into contemporary culture, and passed them on to later ages. Aspects of classical literature appear throughout later literature and philosophy; for example, episodes from Roman history provide the material for plays by Shakespeare, operas by Verdi and novels by Robert Graves. Latin verse and prose styles have been imitated by countless authors, including Pope and Keats in English, and Racine and Molière in French.

Index

Page numbers in italics denote map references.

Acknowledgment

The publishers wish to thank the Museo della Civiltà Romana, Rome, for permission to base the reconstruction of Rome on pages 32-33 of this book on their model of the ancient city.